8. SCANDINAVIAN M...

STORE SKAGASTØLSTIND
from W

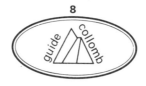

Scandinavian Mountains

PETER LENNON

West Col

SCANDINAVIAN MOUNTAINS

First published in Britain 1987 by
West Col Productions
Goring Reading Berks. RG8 9AA

SBN 906227 32 1

Printed in England by Swindon Press Ltd
Swindon Wilts.

ACKNOWLEDGEMENTS

My thanks are due to Harald Bohne for information; to Finn Hagen for checking the text on Norway and to Tore Abrahamsson for similar on Sweden. Unless otherwise stated in text, illustrations are credited as follows:

Photography, Pat and Peter Lennon

Wildlife and native occupational drawings, Stephanie Collomb

Maps and hut drawings, Pat Lennon

Route diagrams and mountain sketches, Sarah Lennon

Mountain & Wildlife Ventures

Landscape Pathfinders

West Col Productions

Mountain area numbers
corresponding with
contents list opposite

15

17

16

14 18

20
19

13

12

11

10

9
8
5
7
4
6 3 NORWAY
2

1

SWEDEN

Finland

0 50 100 150
                  KM

area key

Contents

goshawk

INTRODUCTION   14

General 14,   Special qualities of Scandinavia 15,   History of
Mountain Developments 18,   Travel to Scandinavia 20,   Inter-
nal Travel – Norway 21,   Internal Travel – Sweden 23,
Mountain Huts – Norway 24,   Mountain Huts – Sweden 25,
Camping – Norway 26,   Camping – Sweden 27,   Climate and
Weather 28,   Equipment 29,   Route grading systems 31,
Glaciers 32,   Maps 33,   Flora and Fauna 34,   The Samers
(or Lapps) 36

7

Illustrations

red-necked phalarope

Nature drawings: goshawk 7, red-necked phalarope 9, honey buzzard 56, red fox 72, elk 80, musk ox 86, great gray owl 93, Samer play sledge and reindeer 100, long-tailed skua 107, wolf 114, red deer 120, white-tailed eagle 134, Samer snow scooter and tent 142, common buzzard 159, shore lark 165, short-tailed vole 185, wolverine 189

ABBREVIATIONS

BA	British Airways
C.	centigrade (temperature)
c.	circa, approximately
CAP	Cappelen (maps). See also Appendix 2
DNT	Norwegian Mountain Touring Association
E	east
ft.	feet
gl.	glacier(s)
h.	hour(s)
kg.	kilograms
km.	kilometre(s)
kmh.	kilometres per hour
L	left
Lat.	latitude
LB	Liber Grafiska (maps). See also Appendix 2
Long.	longitude
M	map scale, representing 1000, eg. 50M = 1/50,000
m.	metres
ml.	miles
mm.	millimetres
N	north
No.	number
NOK	Norwegian Krona (currency)
NTK	Norwegian Alpine Club
pop.	population
pt.	point (spot height)
R	right
S	south
SAS	Scandinavian Airlines
sh.	sheet (map sheet number or name)
SK	Statens Kartverk (Norwegian maps)
SL	Statens Lantmäteriverk (Swedish maps)
sq.	square (measure)
STF	Swedish Touring Club
W	west
YH	youth hostel

4-fig. ref.   4 figure map grid reference
Intermediate compass directions are indicated: SW, NE, etc.

SHORT GLOSSARY

austre	eastern	piggen	sharp ridged peak
botn	cirque or corrie	renne	gully
breen	glacier	ryggen	ridge or ridged
bu	small house or hut	seter	summer farm
dal(en)	valley	skar	steep slope
eggen	edge	skardet	pass
fjell	mountain	stor(a) (e)	big or great
heim	home	søre	southern
hytta	mountain hut or lodge	tind	pointed peak
hø	flat topped mountain	tjåkkå	pointed peak
jåkkå/jokk	fast mountain stream	vagge	valley or way
jaure	lake	vass	water
jekna	glacier	vatn	lake
kaise	king	vatnet	small lake
leden	route or path	veggen	way or road
ligste	lowest	vestre	western
luokta	bay (lake)	vidda	upland plateau
nuten	rounded peak	vik	bay (sea or lake)

Pronunciation of accents

It is useful to have an awareness of the way Scandinavian accents alter the pronunciation of certain words.

Å cap or lower case	pronounced like	aw in paw
Ä as above Swedish		e in pen
Ö as above Swedish		ur in fur
Ø as above Norwegian		as above

MAP SYMBOLS

National Frontier

North

Road number

Lake

Coastal water

Glacier

Mountain summit

Railway and tunnel

Ferry route

Private staffed lodgings

Staffed huts

Self-service huts

Unstaffed huts (Norway)
Huts without provisions (Sweden)

Introduction

General

SCANDINAVIA is normally considered to be composed of Norway – Sweden – Finland – Denmark. For the purposes of this guide book Denmark and Finland have been omitted. Denmark because it has no mountains at all. Finnish Lappland has rolling hills rising to over 1200m., but is considered to have insufficient mountain significance.

Norway and Sweden contain enormous tracts of mountains, exceeding in area the total size of the British Isles. Norway has an area about 125,000 sq.ml. of which no less than 63% is classified mountainous. Sweden, with a total area of 158,000 sq.ml., has about 25%.

The mountains of Scandinavia are poorly documented in the English language. A useful outline touring guide has been produced by the Norwegian Tourist Board for many years; it has always been simplistic and inadequate. The Board also issued a compact climbing guide which went out of print in the 1960s. A climbing guide exists for the Romsdal area, and outline climbing guides were produced to 5 areas in the 1950s, now long out of print.

Surprisingly the publications situation is not much better in the native languages. In Norway a series of detailed touring guides covers only the more popular areas. In 1986 the Norwegian Mountain Touring Association (DNT) produced an outline guide to all areas. Attempts to publish a series of comprehensive mountain guidebooks by the Norwegian Alpine Club (NTK) have got no further than 2 rather expensive and unwieldy volumes to the Hurrungane and Innerdal districts. These contain an English language section. In Sweden there has been touring and ascent literature to all mountain areas in the past, mainly published by the Swedish Touring Club (STF). All are long out of print. At present there is only a good touring and ascent guide to the Sarek National Park; a further volume is planned for the Kebnekaise group.

The purpose of this guide is to fill part of the void. It is not considered practical at present to produce a comprehensive guide to touring and ascent possibilities of such a vast region; merely to offer an outline survey to every important mountain area of Norway and Sweden. Inevitably, some minor areas have had to be excluded. Background information is given for planning a visit to 20 areas. The area divisions may not always coincide with area nominations adopted by others but they are reckoned to be logical and easy to follow.

The descriptions identify the general and special qualities of each area; access, approaches, starting points and bases. All appropriate maps are listed; hut details include type, size and a map reference because some huts are not marked on maps. Under route descriptions a few walking or ski touring itineraries are suggested. Mountain ascents are in the main given in outline form, although selected popular climbs are described more fully.

At present relatively few British walkers, skiers and climbers travel to Scandinavia and these tend to concentrate on a few areas in Norway. It is hoped that the guidebook will awaken interest in the other areas and in the great potential, not just for new climbing routes but also for exciting and enjoyable experiences in remote wilderness areas.

Special qualities of Scandinavia

For those accustomed to crowded British or Alpine areas, the Scandinavian mountains will seem empty. Only the short Easter hut opening times attract crowds and these are confined to a few areas.

Swedish Lappland, Arctic Norway, the immense Børgefjell border area N of Trondheim are incredibly remote by European standards. It is possible to go for days without seeing another person; this is attractive for those seeking solitude, but hazardous in the event of accident.

There is a strong touring tradition in Scandinavia, on foot in summer and by ski in winter. For some reason few people are interested in ascents and the number of active climbers is small. Nevertheless, the few have achieved some outstanding routes and exploration continues. This general lack of interest in ascents does contribute to the untrodden feeling on many peaks and climbs. Even in an area as popular as the Jotunheimen in summer the author has climbed for a week and only met other parties on 2 mountains; though at the same time numerous tourers were passing through the valleys and over passes.

One of the most refreshing aspects of a visit to Scandinavia is the friendly attitude of both Norwegians and Swedes, particularly towards British visitors. This is partly due to the lack of a language barrier; English is their second language and is learned in school from the age of 9 or 10. There are historical reasons too, as British climbers played an important part in the early developments of climbing in Norway. Also links between Norway and Britain during the Second World War strengthen this affinity.

Culturally there are strong similarities between the Scandinavians and the British. Among other things we share many of the same expressions and even jokes, when translated. Norse is integrated with Anglo-

Saxon to form part of the modern English language. It is easy to feel at home with people who live such a similar lifestyle.

Another factor is the natural friendliness and generosity of the people. It would be invidious to make comparisons between Norwegians and Swedes as both are equally hospitable, although their initial response may vary. As most hill-travellers abroad will be aware, this state of friendly co-operation is rare in mountain areas today. It is something that must be preserved and this can easily be achieved by exercising a little commonsense and reasonable behaviour.

For British visitors there are reciprocal health agreements with Norway and Sweden. In the unlucky event of falling sick or being hospitalised through accident, the charge is a nominal one. In many countries now mountain rescue can be an expensive experience. All rescue in Scandinavia is normally free, but very expensive recoveries in doubtful circumstances (parachuting down the Troll Wall) have resulted in some costs being passed on. In Sweden rescue services are carried out by the police, mainly using helicopters. In Norway the police also co-ordinate rescue usually in close co-operation with specialist Red Cross rescue volunteers, all of whom are climbers. Such groups exist in Oslo, Bergen, Sunnmøre, Romsdal, Trondheim, Svolvaer and Tromsø. It is worth remembering at all times that rescue in isolated areas can take a long time.

For the mountain visitor Scandinavia offers an unrivalled variety of terrain. The general mountaineer is spoiled for choice by thousands of interesting summits, some remote, some easily accessible; from the savage rocky islands of Lofoten and the Norwegian Arctic coast to the lonely tops of Sarek National Park in Swedish Lappland. Glaciers, in all sizes, may emanate from large ice-caps. Many ascents can be tried by walkers, while others require rock climbing and some involve glacier crossings. Although there are high standard modern climbs, the majority of mountain routes are in the low to middle grades.

For the pure rock climber Norway has routes of all standards and lengths up to the 2000m. of Romsdal. Huge stretches of untouched rock remain, much of it at lower levels, such as the endless slabs and walls of the sea fjords. In many places the rock is superb granite. In winter hundreds of frozen waterfalls in Norway and Sweden offer ice-climbing at all standards. In winter Scandinavia is in a class of its own. Its northern geographic and climatic situation results in long winters and reliable snow cover. Mountain ski-touring, either from hut to hut or camping, allows access to even the most remote sectors. Simply travelling through the mountains by ski is a wonderful experience, but combining winter ascents with touring has much greater potential.

GLITTERTIND summit

One last feature, unique in Europe, must be mentioned. In summer the northern latitudes mean long hours of daylight. Even the southern and central ranges have such long hours that benightment is not a serious problem in June and July. Further N in districts along and beyond the Arctic Circle, you are truly in the "Land of the Midnight Sun". Here, with no darkness for several weeks, the northern summer has a special timeless quality. Day and night no longer mean the same as in lower latitudes. It is not uncommon to find people out fishing at 2 am, or to see climbers setting out for a long route at 4 pm. Some find the permanent light disturbing, but others are drawn back year after year to re-experience the unique qualities of the Scandinavian northlands.

History of Mountain Developments

The earliest mountain exploration was carried out by the Samer people (Lapps). In summer their reindeer wander far and wide and can sometimes be found high on the more rounded tops. The herders were familiar with nearly all aspects of the mountains, and this is reflected in their picturesque and descriptive names which are found throughout Norwegian and Swedish Lappland. Only glaciers remained unnamed and presumably untrodden.

Further S and much later, particularly in the high central regions of Norway, farmer-hunters wandered the mountains in search of game. They were sometimes employed by the early questing botanists and other naturalists who sought the secrets of the mountains. The great Swedish naturalist Carl Linnaeus has left us fascinating accounts of his wilderness journeys in the 18th century.

The first records of mountain ascents occur in the late 18th and early 19th century. In Norway of the highest pair, Glittertind was ascended by 1842 (H N Wergeland, H Sletten) and Galdhøpiggen by 1844 (B M Keilhau and surveyor Andresen). Earlier ascents were recorded on Snøhetta in 1796 by surveyor J Esmark and party; Sulitjelma in 1807 by G Wahlenberg. Surprisingly in the rugged Hurrungane, Nordre Skagastølstind by C P B Boeck, B M Keilhau; and Nordre Dyrhaugstind by G Bohr – both in 1820. Romsdalhorn in 1828 by Hans Bjermeland and Christen Hoel; on Arctic Seiland island, the Seiland gl. was mounted in 1826 by Robert Everest, B M Keilau. Exploration in Sweden was later, probably because of the great difficulties of access to Lappland.

Paralleling developments in the Alps, the second half of the 19th century saw a dramatic increase in the rate of exploration. This era heralded the emergence of mountain activities as we see them now. Many famous mountaineers visited Scandinavia, but especially Norway, and some became captivated by its unique qualities. In Norway, Cecil Slingsby returned year after year exploring almost all the chief areas and putting up some magnificent climbs, usually in the company of Norwegian friends and guides.

The Norwegian Mountain Touring Association (DNT) was founded in 1868, with regional touring associations appearing about 1880. At this time there was no division in mountaineering and touring; mountain guides were long associated with DNT. Huts were constructed by DNT and by private owners, a number of whom were themselves early guides. By the end of the century improved access and accommodation had encouraged an ever growing number of mountain tourists.

In Sweden the mountains of Lappland were at that time extremely remote. The railways and hydro-electric power stations and roads were yet to come. It could take days to travel from the Baltic coast into Sarek or Kebnekaise. The most significant early ascent was that of Sarektjåkkå (2089m.) in 1879 by the cartographer G W Bucht. In other districts, particularly in the Jämtland border highlands, the surveyors were often the pioneers. The French mountaineer and explorer Charles Rabot made the first ascent of the highest peak, Kebnekaise South Top (2117m.) in 1883; surprisingly he had ascended the more remote Sarektjåkkå two years earlier. From 1895 Axel Hamberg visited the Sarek area to begin his long geological, meteorological and biological studies which were to last more than 35 years.

The Swedish Touring Club (STF) was founded in 1885, but no huts were constructed in the Lappland mountains until 1904, though huts had been built in the more southerly ranges.

The first half of the 20th century brought about steady exploration and development of new climbs of more difficulty. In Norway the previous British interest gradually waned and most routes were produced by Norwegians. The Norwegian Alpine Club (NTK) was established in 1908 and soon enacted a strict code of mountain ethics. Similarly, Swedish climbers were responsible for the vast majority of new routes, with the occasional incursion of German and other foreign mountaineers. The 2 national touring associations greatly extended their hut chains, with local clubs in Norway adding their contribution to the network. Marked trails appeared in the more popular areas; walking and ski-touring became increasingly popular.

More recently there was a great upsurge of activity when the scope for great wall climbs in Romsdal was realised. This led to an international scramble for prestige routes and even a short lived formation of a corps of Romsdal guides. Since then the quest for new routes has been left very much to native climbers. Proliferation of local climbing clubs in both countries has resulted in more specialised rock climbing and a growing interest in the multitude of low level crags which abound in Norway. In winter waterfall and other ice climbing is advancing rapidly.

TRAVEL TO SCANDINAVIA

Air Routes: There are regular scheduled flights from Britain to Norway and Sweden operated by SAS, BA, Dan Air, Air UK.

London, Manchester and Glasgow to Stavanger, Bergen, Oslo, Gothenburg, Stockholm.

Newcastle to Stavanger, Bergen, Oslo. Aberdeen to Stavanger, Bergen.

Normal scheduled fares are expensive, but a number of special fares are available. These are of the Apex type and are normally restricted to certain dates and flights, and minimum and maximum stays; they require up to one month advance payment in full and carry heavy cancellation or alteration penalties. In winter flying provides the only direct routes to most of Norway, although there is a recent sea route from Harwich to Oslo.

Sea Crossings: These have been subjected to much alteration of ship operators, routes, times and prices. At one stage it appeared as if DFDS would secure a total monopoly, but currently Fred Olsen and Norway Line have operations too. The future seems equally uncertain, with the probable summer situation as follows:

Newcastle to Stavanger and Bergen, 3 x weekly May-October 21-25 h.
Newcastle to Gothenburg, 2 x weekly June-September 26-28 h.
Harwich to Kristiansand and Oslo, 1 x weekly All Year 36 h.
Harwich to Gothenburg, 4 x weekly June-September; 3 x weekly All Year 22-25 h.

Prices vary enormously between different operators and at different seasons. In general the short summer season July/August has very high prices. For individuals planning to use public transport in Scandinavia it is often cheaper to fly. In winter ship prices are considerably lower and offer good value. The modern ships out of Harwich are fully stabilised and comfortable in virtually all weather conditions.

At all times there are a number of special self-catering chalet/camping package deals giving good discounts from normal fares. On all crossings cars are usually transported free with 4 or more paying passengers, but minibuses and other large vehicles/trailers are subject to varying surcharges. Most routes give group discounts (for 10+) and varying youth group rates, again for 10+. These are normally only available for the cheapest on-board accommodation.

Rail (and Short Sea): An alternative from the South of England is to take either Harwich-Hook of Holland, or Dover-Ostend to start. Then Hook of Holland-Stockholm by rail in

24h; onward train to Lappland, add 18h. Or Ostend-Gothenburg in 23h; add 5h. to Oslo and a further 18h. to Fauske for Arctic Norway. The main advantage seems to be with the under 26 age group using an Interail Pass.

Bus (and Short Sea): There are bus links to major cities in Norway and Sweden from London (Victoria Coach Station) via the Channel crossings. These services are normally only available from June to September. Prices are below peak North Sea crossing rates, but unless you are a bus enthusiast it would seem a tedious way of travelling.

INTERNAL TRAVEL - NORWAY

Air: There is an extensive network of internal air routes in Norway. These can be expedient for mountain travellers going to the far North, who are short of time (but not money). The fare structure is, as always, complex. While normally expensive, there are some cheaper deals, especially for families in the summer season. For unusually remote areas it is possible to charter small aircraft fitted with floats or skis. For a group this can be reasonably priced.

Coastal Ship: All year round a ship leaves Bergen daily bound for Kirkenes. This world famous journey (Hurtigruten) is of great interest and outstanding beauty. Regretably it is also a world leader in exorbitant pricing, if one is to travel complete with cabin and food. However, it should still be possible to go as a deck passenger, when it would afford useful access to some of the Fjord ranges and parts of Arctic Norway.

Rail: The system is fairly limited though useful for access to quite a number of mountain areas. The main lines are from Oslo to Bergen; Oslo to Stavanger; Oslo to Trondheim; Trondheim to Bodø. There are also important links with Sweden into Trondheim and Narvik. Fares are similar to British, with cheap mid-week tickets and group rates. Mid-week tickets are good value on longer journeys.

Bus: An extensive network of bus services exists throughout Norway, although in some areas services are infrequent. Nearly all major towns are linked by express bus. For medium to large groups (18+) very flexible charter services and rates are available. In Arctic Norway bus services are usually well coordinated to other transport systems and give access to quite remote areas. A number of services use postbuses. In winter some services are unable to run in many mountain areas; it is wise to inquire locally, as weather conditions are very variable. At Easter there are a number of special ski buses, particularly from Oslo into the Jotunheimen and other popular skiing areas. Information from DNT head office. In addition numerous snowmobiles offer bus or taxi services to some huts.

Road: During the summer period all mountain areas are accessible by road, though some high passes and minor roads can remain blocked by snow until mid June. Generally speaking the mountain road system is not of a high quality. In the mountain areas of the S and W roads are often very narrow, steep and poorly surfaced with tight and continuous bends. In the N it is uncommon to drive on tarmac away from the E6 highway or out of built up areas. Unmade roads can be hard on suspension and there is danger to headlights and screens from stones. The final sections up to some mountain starting points can be on private toll roads, often with a bad surface and expensive to use.

Petrol is more expensive than in Britain. Filling stations are reasonably frequent in most southern/western areas, but infrequent in the N. Many close early, particularly at weekends. A small but growing number on main through roads have 24 h. automat pumps, paid for by 10 or 100 NOK bank notes.

In the peak summer months the population of Norway is virtually doubled by the influx of tourists. This can cause long delays at overworked garages in case of breakdowns. Garages are usually helpful to British drivers, but a comprehensive spares kit is advisable. Distances to the mountains of the Arctic are great. Oslo to Tromsø is nearly 1800 km. (more than 1100 ml.). Allow at least 3 days in the peak season.

Maximum speed limits are low, normally 80 kmh. In practice large stretches of road are restricted to 70 kmh. or even 60 kmh. Towns are 50 down to 30 kmh. During peak times main through routes such as the E6 are severely congested. Norwegians ordinarily are slow drivers and the police are very hard on speed offenders.

Winter driving in Norway presents many problems. In mountain areas it is obligatory to have studded tyres or chains and most mountain roads are subject to at least temporary closure through snow. Temperatures in Arctic Norway are low, but it is not often realised that they can be very low elsewhere. Voss has recorded -50 C. in recent years. Vehicles must be prepared accordingly.

Ferries and other Sea Routes: The coastline is deeply indented with several major fjords and many minor ones which break up the continuity of the road system. In most places ferries run frequently and for many hours of the day, but there can be delays on popular crossings. Beware of being benighted. There are express and and slower services on Sognefjord and Nordfjord in particular, and good access to several mountain groups. Lofoten and Vesterålen islands are served by a series of medium duration and short services. Full details of main ferry/other sea route times and prices are produced annually by the Norwegian Tourist Office. In addition there are useful access boats operating on the mountain lakes of Gjende, Bygdin and Femund. Details from DNT.

INTERNAL TRAVEL - SWEDEN

Air: An extensive network of internal routes operates mostly in lowland areas. Good flight connections to Kiruna and Gällivare in Lappland. Scheduled prices are expensive, with some summer season family fares at reasonable rates. Some stand-by fares for under-26 year olds to and from Stockholm at low rates. In mountain areas there are some seasonal scheduled local float plane and helicopter services, also charter services. Some are reasonably priced and provide useful access for otherwise difficult areas.

Rail: Swedish Rail (SJ) has a few lines useful for mountain travellers. The main line joining Östersund with Trondheim and the minor inland line both give access to the Central Border region. In Lappland the main line through Gällivare and Kiruna continues to the frontier and eventually Narvik. The minor inland line goes through Jokkmokk, Porjus and other useful jumping-off points.

Some years ago the Swedes made a bold experiment by offering greatly reduced fares to special Low Price Card holders, except on Fridays and Sundays. Families received automatic reductions on all days. The result was very busy trains with advance booking essential. Since the beginning of 1986 this has been abandoned in favour of a confused system of ticketing mainly with higher prices.

Bus: Express services link most major towns and give access to some mountain areas. Local services, sometimes postbuses, give excellent access to many remote areas, often at subsidised prices. Some of these local services operate for only a short season; contact local tourist offices for current information.

Boat: In some parts of Lappland small boats provide regular services on lakes and large rivers deep in the mountain areas. Prices are often reasonable. Times and dates available vary greatly; details from STF direct.

Road: Swedish mountain areas in the main are more remote than those of Norway. This means fewer road links, but these are invariably better, faster and open virtually all year. Few mountain roads are closed by snow. The ordinary road system throughout is excellent, and while there are few motorways there are many dual carriageways. The normal roads are remarkably wide and straight; maximum speed limits 110 kmh. It is tempting to drive faster on such roads, and some do, but speed traps (radar, even helicopters) are fairly common and penalties severe.

Distances to northern areas are great; it is over 1600 km. (1000 ml.) from Gothenburg to Sarek National Park, about 2 days driving. For winter driving in the mountain areas studded tyres are a great advantage. Otherwise chains should be carried. In midwinter and what is known in Lappland as "spring-winter", temperatures can be low, even below -45C, and vehicles should be prepared accordingly.

Tourist traffic is less heavy than in Norway. Breakdowns and repairs can be expected to be sorted out fairly quickly, even in summer peak times. Filling stations in mountain areas are thinly spread.

MOUNTAIN HUTS - NORWAY

About 250 huts can be used by walkers, climbers, skiers, all loosely coordinated into a network by the Norwegian Touring Association, better known as DNT. DNT was formed in 1868 and directly operates a minority of the hut network; it also marks summer and winter trails, and provides information on hut opening dates/capacity/type/status/prices, etc. Huts are also owned by several regional touring associations, and others are privately owned - especially in the Jotunheimen.

Huts are not evenly distributed throughout Norway; the majority are in the southern and central areas, with only a few in the N. For the Lofoten & Vesterålen Islands the only huts available are Rorbuer, the simple buildings of fishermen. On the Finnmarksvidda huts known as 'Fjellstue' are owned by the state.

There are 3 types of mountain hut in the DNT system, as follows.

Staffed Huts: Large huts and several have more than 100 bedspaces. The majority of private huts within the network are of this type; some of them are really hotels with all conceivable facilities including sauna and swimming pool. They are expensive. A full meal service is normally provided; self catering is not usually allowed. However, some DNT huts have a self-service area which can be used out of the main season. Many huts of this type are only open for a short winter season, sometimes as little as 10 days at Easter. In the summer season they are open for as little as 6 weeks. They are not usually accessible by the DNT standard key.

Self-service hut: Often smaller and less sophisticated than staffed huts; should be fully equipped with gas cooker, wood burning stove/s, kitchen equipment and utensils, also a variety of provisions for sale. Bunks with blankets, normally clean and comfortable - vastly superior to many Alpine huts. Many huts are wardened during the peak seasons. Out of season they are normally closed with the standard DNT lock. Some regional associations have different arrangements and should always be contacted in advance.

All huts have a safe box and specially printed envelopes to hold your payment and details of accommodation and provisions bought. Please remember that the continuation of this convenient type of hut system is dependent on your honesty. Members prices are about the same as the highest category British youth hostels. At least one person in any group using the huts must be a DNT member.

Unstaffed hut: Usually fairly small, but in most other respects identical to self-service huts. No warden, no provisions and huts are normally locked. Prices and terms are the same as self-service huts.

Membership: Members obtain large discounts in self-service and unstaffed huts, also smaller discounts in the staffed ones. There are reciprocal rights with regional associations, private huts and the Swedish Touring Association (STF) huts. No reciprocal rights with the UIAA European system. Members can obtain standard keys from Oslo by sending a deposit. Application forms from: DNT, Postboks 1963 Vika, 0125 Oslo. See also page 192.

MOUNTAIN HUTS - SWEDEN

This system differs from the Norwegian in that virtually all huts in the network are directly controlled by the national organisation - Swedish Touring Association (STF). It also controls the extensive YH system. STF is a larger, somewhat bureaucratic and less efficient organisation than DNT, and is now partly subsidised by the Swedish state. There are less than 100 huts in total; in contrast to Norway these are mainly in northern areas. Normally a section in each hut remains open all year round. Huts are wardened or fully staffed during the winter and summer seasons. There are 2 types of hut.

Staffed hut: Known as 'fjällstation', these are larger huts, several with over 100 bedspaces, usually a choice of accommodation and normally supplying a full meal service. One or two are now becoming self-catering only and most allow some self-catering in a separate building. Provisions and sometimes fuel (Trangia spirit) are for sale; often there is a telephone (direct line or radio). Hut and meal prices are higher and rising faster than in the DNT system, in spite of Sweden having lower prices and a lower inflation rate than Norway.

Self-service hut: Some are quite large, approaching 100 places and the trend is now to build self-service huts only. These new huts are often equipped extravagantly – one was recently reconstructed for a cost exceeding one million pounds. However the majority are small to medium size, well designed and equipped with gas cooker, wood burning stove, catering equipment and blankets, etc. Provisions are not normally available, except in a few locations; these will be indicated in the relevant areas. Huts are wardened for longer periods than in Norway – it should be noted that wardens are usually helpful and friendly.

Membership: Members receive a modest discount in huts. It is not necessary to be a member to use any hut, but membership also allows reciprocal rights in Norwegian huts, as well as youth hostels. Application forms from: STF, Stureplan 2, Box 7615, 10394 Stockholm.

CAMPING – NORWAY

Camping is either on the organised, constructed site (several hundred) or at an independent free site, usually found in the mountains. Organised sites are mainly in valleys and coastal areas, with very few in the mountains. A feature in many sites is the camping hut with small, fairly basic facilities for sleeping and cooking, which can often be rented for one night – useful on long journeys to the Arctic areas, particularly if the weather is bad.

Sites are classified in 3 grades. Charges are made per vehicle and tent with additional charges per person. Prices are chiefly controlled by the Norwegian Automobile Association (NAF), who also publish a handbook of sites. Details from: NAF, Storgaten 2, Oslo 1.

There is a long established tradition of independent camping in Norway, especially in the mountains – a tradition consolidated by the 1957 Great Open Air Charter. In this you may not camp within 100m. of a mountain hut or other inhabited building, but otherwise in mountain

areas you are allowed to camp freely. This right also carries the responsibility to leave the site tidy and clean. Since 1983 there has been
some "legal" distortion of the Charter in popular mountain areas such
as the Jotunheimen and Rondane. Here you are now forbidden to camp
closer than one km. from huts or inhabited buildings. Alternative sites
have been established close to huts on a charge basis.

CAMPING - SWEDEN

There is a choice between organised sites and independent camping. In
the annual camping book produced by the Swedish Tourist Board more
than 500 authorised sites are listed. There are few organised sites in
mountain areas. Swedish sites come in 3 grades. Prices are lower than
in Norway and charges are per pitch. For once this is an advantage to
the mountain camper with small tents. Organised sites are useful on
longer journeys to Lappland, as it is not always easy to find suitable
independent sites en route.

Independent camping is widely allowed in lowland as well as mountain
areas. The Swedish Allmansrätten gives the right of access and one
night camping almost everywhere away from inhabited buildings, protected areas and growing crops. This is a responsibility as well as a
right and irresponsible behaviour in some popular localities is increasing pressure for new restrictions. In mountain areas no problems arise
with independent camping. It is possible to camp close to huts if you
wish to use their facilities; this carries a moderate charge.

General Points: The vast expanses of Norway and Sweden give
almost unlimited backpacking scope, both on
foot and on ski. There are a number of important differences to backpacking in Britain and the rest of Europe. Many mountain regions are
remote. This means that it is difficult or even impossible to replenish
fuel and food en route. A much greater degree of self-sufficiency is
required. Campers/backpackers are not entitled to buy food at the huts,
even if they are members of DNT/STF, although this is often allowed.

Choice of cooker is important as fuel supplies can be a problem, even
in medium size towns. Camping gas is uncommon or rare; paraffin is
difficult to locate in shops, but (in Norway) may sometimes be available from filling stations. Trangia spirit is most common, although it
is extremely expensive in Norway - about 5 times the price of petrol.
Note, fuel must not be carried on aircraft.

Other camping problems include insect pests. Midges though not as
common as in Scotland can be a nuisance in some years. Mosquitoes
are a pest in the wetter valleys everywhere, except the Fjord ranges;

and a major irritation in parts of Lappland, though numbers vary annually. Insects diminish with altitude, but can be found up to 1500m. Buy local repellants, carry Piriton tablets to alleviate any reaction and don't wear shorts.

Winter camping in Scandinavia requires good equipment and serious forethought. December, January and February have short days, often stormy weather and very low temperatures – worse for example than the Cairngorms. From March camping becomes more practical and good ski backpacking can be enjoyed, in some areas, well into May.

CLIMATE AND WEATHER

The mountain areas of Norway and Sweden extend over many degrees of latitude. The Rogaland/Setesdal Highlands lie around 59 N, while the far northern ranges of Arctic Norway virtually reach 70 N. This inevitably results in considerable climatic variations, perhaps best shown in the tree line and the lower limit of glaciers, both varying by several hundred metres between S and N. Comparing sea-level temperatures, Bergen has a mean in January of 1.5 C, while Tromsø averages -3.5 C. Similar differences are found in the mountains, although to some extent this is disguised by the existence of higher mountains in southern areas. All time extremes of cold are little different N to S; both Karasjok and Voss have recorded -51 C.

The long, basically N-S axis of the Scandinavian mountains to a great extent forms the division between the maritime and continental climatic regions, producing large temperature and precipitation differences. However, some Atlantic depressions force their way through the W-E passes, bringing milder moist air. January mean temperature in the Nordmore mountain area of the Fjord ranges is -4.5 C, whereas the uplands of N Dalarna average -12 C. Precipitation shows even greater contrasts with Bergen having 3150mm. annually against eastern Sweden with less than 400mm.

The winter climate overall is remarkably milder than other countries at similar latitudes – for 2 important reasons. Firstly, a branch of the Gulf Stream passes up the W coast of Norway and round into Russia. This warmflow maintains mainly ice-free conditions in Norwegian ports, allowing an all year coastal ship service to link communities which often have all or part of their road system blocked by snow. The influence of this warmer water is only felt inland for a few km. Then more important for maintaining higher land temperatures are Atlantic depressions, mainly tracking in from the SW and carrying vast quantities of warm, moist air in their circulation. Naturally this affects the W and SW most, but influences all Scandinavia to some extent. Average January temperatures at 65 N in Swedish Lappland are -22 C, compared to say Canada -32 C, and Siberia -37 C at the same latitudes.

The summer season is relatively short with considerable variations, both N to S and W to E. Generally most mountain areas in the S and Central regions are usable for walking and climbing by mid June. Arctic areas can be very wet with meltwater until the beginning or even the middle of July. Arctic areas and summits over 1800m. anywhere can have snowfalls in any month. Over simplified, it is normally wetter in the S and W, drier in the E and NE, but there are many localised variations. Long hours of daylight - in some Arctic areas 24h. for some weeks - when routes can be attempted round the clock - help to compensate for prolonged rainy periods. Not all summers are wet by any means; some are characterised by long dry periods.

Winter mountain visitors must expect very variable weather conditions. Until March storms occur at times almost everywhere and are particularly violent in western areas. The weather station on the summit of Fannaråken (2062m.) in the Hurrungane district of the Jotunheimen has recorded gale force winds on about 35% of days in November-February, with significant snowfall on 20 days each of the same months. High pressure conditions are more common later in the winter and spring, sometimes lasting for long periods. April and May can be outstanding in some years, giving excellent skiing and even good rock climbing on S facing ridges and walls.

EQUIPMENT

Walking: Walkers require similar clothing and equipment as for summer walking in the Scottish Highlands. Boots should not be lightweight and should be as waterproof as possible. Long rubberised boots are used by many Scandinavians, very useful for wet areas, but not suitable for ascents. Temperatures above 1000m. are generally lower than in Britain, especially in Arctic areas where it can freeze at lower altitudes, even in midsummer. Gloves and balaclava should be carried. Mountain rivers and streams can be a serious hazard, notably in Arctic areas where there are few bridges. Sarek National Park is notorious for its rapidly changing river levels. A lightweight rope, or preferably 2, and practice in river crossings is a wise precaution.

Camping - Summer: A good mountain tent is essential, preferably with plenty of space, such as the modern dome or tunnel types. To camp at higher levels a valance is useful as you may be forced to camp on snow or boulderfields, where pegging is impractical. Then a karrimat and a sleeping bag good for temperatures down to -5 C are needed. On stony ground it is sometimes necessary to put karrimats under the groundsheet. Carry a good repair kit and be as self-sufficient as possible. It is virtually impossible to replace equipment in most areas.

Camping - Winter: All equipment must be first class. Loss of a tent through storm in the night would have serious consequences. Modern "expedition-quality" dome and tunnel tents have proved reliable, although expensive. Snow pegs/anchors can be useful, while skis, sticks or ice axes will act as guy anchors. Snow shovels are essential for site preparation, snow wall and emergency shelter construction and snow clearance in prolonged storms. Most gas cookers fail to work in low temperatures. Additional fuel is needed for snow melting; allow double summer usage. Sleeping bags should be good for -30C; down is still the best and can be protected from condensation by a goretex bivvy bag.

Climbing: It is difficult to generalise because climbing varies greatly from area to area. Most districts require walking approaches measured in hours rather than minutes, and many ordinary routes have less continuous climbing. Good general mountaineering boots seem best for most situations. Rock boots are used on outlying crags and have been used on some of the long Romsdal walls, but are worthless for long approaches.

A single 9mm or 11mm x 40m. rope is adequate for climbing up to grade IV; above this use your own preference. Long abseils are uncommon, except in case of retreat on big walls. Many areas have loose rock and helmets are advised. Belays can sometimes be a problem, so that "Friends" are extremely useful and a variety of runner sizes should be carried.

Snow climbing possibilities are limited by the curious characteristics of Scandinavian snow conditions. In summer near permanent daylight usually means little or no night frost with often suspect snow. In the winter temperatures remain consistently below freezing for long periods, in places resulting in unconsolidated snow until spring. Frozen waterfalls offer great winter potential, with interest in Norway rapidly growing. A single normal length ice axe, crampons and belay equipment are adequate for general snow/ice mountaineering. The ice climbing specialist should carry the full armoury.

Skiing: Long cold winters and about 100,000 sq. ml. of fine skiable mountain terrain offer almost unlimited potential for touring. Recent improvements in Nordic ski equipment and techniques have widened the possibilities further with Nordic ski mountaineering as a practical application. Nordic mountain skis are broader and stronger, with light camber, good sidecut and steel edges. They give good glide in level and undulating ground, but can also descend medium steep slopes. Telemark turns have enjoyed a renewal of popularity; stem and parallel turns can be executed on improved equipment, given the right snow conditions. Boots have been stiffened and are available with vibram soles, capable of taking crampons and obviating the need for a second pair of heavy boots. Lightweight 3-pin toe bindings have now been strengthened to give greater reliability, but cable bindings are still more popular in Scandinavia.

Spare ski tips, repair kits and snow shovels should form part of touring equipment. For long tours and camping expeditions a special plastic or wooden towing sledge (called a pulk) is very useful to reduce rucsac weights, or extend the range of a tour.

ROUTE GRADING SYSTEMS

Walking: In Norway mountain walking route distances are normally given in hours. As many routes have to gain or lose considerable height, this is a practical measurement. In Sweden mountain walking route distances are shown in km. Some Swedish areas are less steep than Norwegian, which perhaps explains the difference, though it is not an adequate guide for steeper areas.

Swedish National Parks: Because of the remote and serious nature of some northern National Parks, it was decided for safety reasons to give the Parks a grading from 1 to 6. Thus Sarek is 6, Padjelanta 4 and Stora Sjöfallet 4. Despite this many people still underestimate the difficulties of travelling in these areas where at times it is possible to be 4 days march from the nearest road (and assistance).

Climbing: Attempting to grade climbs in Scandinavia has caused great problems. Norway and Sweden sometimes use the same system, but there are many inconsistencies and a total absence of grading at times. Moreover there is very little existing literature and a reluctance among climbers to divulge route details. The author has tried to verify the grading of climbs, but with the exception of a few areas, routes are so poorly documented that a cross reference has not been generally possible. A pioneering attitude and good judgement is required. It is a mountain region with a great deal of new route potential. Mostly route descriptions are of the outline type, as detailed information does not exist for most areas. An ungraded ascent may not necessarily be only a walk or scramble, so be prepared. In almost all areas it is worth remembering that climbs are not repeated with anything like the same frequency as in Britain or the Alps, so there are few signs of use or wear.

Official Norwegian gradings are in 2 parts; overall route and rock pitch:

Grade I   Mainly scrambling, rope may be necessary
      II   Easy climbs, pitches up to 3
     III   Mainly 3, but may include pitches of 4
     IV   Mainly 4, but in some areas, and on shorter routes, up to 5+
      V   Mainly 5, with up to 6 included
     VI   Mainly 6, but with 6+ possible
    VI+   6 and 6+, often sustained; long artificial sections.

Pitch gradings - British equivalents:

1/2	Up to Difficult	5	Very Severe
3	Very Difficult	6	Hard Very Severe
4	Severe	6+	Extremely Severe (no attempt to grade within this)

More often than not only one grade is given for Norwegian routes and it is not always possible to be sure if this is an overall route grade or hardest pitch grade. For safety reasons these routes have been qualified with the overall grade number.

Swedish gradings tend to be mainly of the 1 to 6 type, usually applied by the hardest pitch on the route. This system is quite adequate with fewer climbing areas in Sweden and no really long serious routes requiring more complicated double gradings.

GLACIERS

With the continued apparent amelioration of the climate, the Scandinavian glaciers are shrinking and causing problems to mountain users. Immediately below some valley glaciers there is an area of mud and unstable boulders, often perched on an isolated platform of old ice. Upper Riingsdalen in the Hurrungane district of the Jotunheimen is particularly notorious and there have been several accidents. On glaciers themselves crevasses have opened up on routes used regularly by walkers and skiers, long considered to be virtually without risk. Ice falls have become more difficult and cirque glaciers have seen increased sérac falls. Established glacier approaches to some rock routes fall short by many metres, leaving a dangerous area of ice-smoothed rock often with loose and precarious debris.

Climbers should be able to assess these hazards adequately. Because many valley and ice cap glaciers are used as through routes by walkers and skiers, glacier guides are available whose charges are moderate and advice free. If you are a walker and plan to cross a glacier, obtain up to date particulars first.

MAPS

Norway: Survey maps are issued by Statens Kartverk - SK (formerly Norsk Geografiske Oppmåling - NGO) who also distribute the maps of Norsk Polarinstitutt (Svalbard and Antarctic areas); also Vassdragsdirektoratet (Glacier maps, Depths/Lakes maps and Hydrographic maps). Maps are produced in a wide range of scales from 1:25,000 to 1:1,000,000 and consist of Topographic, Touring, Aeronautical and Thematic series.

For many years Norway had an unenviable reputation for poor quality topographic maps for outdoor users. This situation is being remedied with the introduction of a 4 colour 1:50,000 series, with 20m. contour intervals, to cover all Norway by 1989. Maps required within each area and details about the new series are given in the guide. The old series is available for areas not yet covered by the new. The latter are 2-colour with 50m. contour intervals; they are poor and difficult to use. A 1:100,000 series also covers most of the old series areas and is actually clearer.

Cappelen of Oslo (CAP) produce a number of excellent quality, large format maps at 1:325,000 and 1:400,000. These are invaluable for general planning and travelling. They are updated regularly whereas SK maps are not revised for years - even the newer series. Geological maps are available for a limited number of areas.

Sweden: Survey maps are issued by Statens Lantmäteriverk (SL), who also distribute the New Mountain Series and general touring maps issued by the commercial publisher Liber Grafiska (LB). Maps come in numerous scales. Economic at 1:10,000 and 1:20,000; Topographic at 1:50,000 and 1:100,000; special touring from 1:20,000 to 1:250,000; regional and aeronautical from 1:500,000 to 1:1,000,000. All maps are of high quality. 1:50,000 topo maps have 5m. contour intervals, 1:100,000 maps 20m. intervals.

Liber New Mountain series (Nya Fjällkarten) are at 1:50,000 and at 1:100,000; contour intervals are at 10m. and 20m. respectively, and all show excellent detail and are easy to use. These maps also have superimposed mountain information including marked trails (winter and summer), emergency shelters and telephones, huts and bridges. These maps will shortly be phased out and replaced by a similar series of mountain maps at 1:100,000 to be published by SL. Liber regional touring maps at 1:250,000 and 1:300,000 are reasonably satisfactory for general planning and travelling. Esselte also produce a regional series at 1:300,000. Geological maps cover a limited number of areas. Note in the guidebook text abbreviations used for map scales, eg 50M, 100M. etc. = 1:50,000, 1:100,000 etc.

FLORA AND FAUNA

The mountain flowers of Scandinavia have long been renowned. It is interesting to note that some of the earliest explorers of mountain areas in both Norway and Sweden were botanists. The most famous was Carl Linnaeus who travelled through Lappland (Norway, as well as Sweden) in 1732 to study its natural history (and people) for the Uppsala University Academy of Sciences. He travelled 6000 km. (3800 ml.) in five months, mainly alone.

It is a comparatively short time since ice covered virtually the whole of the Scandinavian mountains, certainly excluding most forms of plant life from vast areas. As the ice receded recolonisation has been rapid and a surprisingly rich and varied mountain flora has developed. There are approximately 250 species of flowering plants. Considerable controversy exists regarding the period when these flowers migrated to Scandinavia and from where they came. Some are Arctic flowers and have returned from the South; others are Arctic plants and some believe these have spread from ice-free "islands" remaining throughout the last ice age.

Mountain flowers are noted for their outstanding beauty, although this is probably enhanced by the wonderful situations where they are to be found. Many botanists consider them to be the most attractive of all plants and the Scandinavian mountain flora is no exception. The subject is covered by a useful reference book: Mountain Flowers by Olav Gjaerovell and Reidar Jorgensen, illustrated by Dagne Tande Lid. The areas of botanic importance are indicated within the main text.

European mammals are well represented and in some cases are thriving. Probably the most successful species is the elk, widespread in forest areas and now found in very large numbers in parts of Sweden, particularly Värmland province. A population explosion has occurred since changes in forest management and the imposition of hunting restrictions.

Being a herd animal, reindeer are locally common and sometimes congregate in their hundreds, unlike the more solitary elk. Wild reindeer are most common in S Norway, notably with large numbers on Hardangervidda. They can be found in the higher mountains, sometimes above 2000m., foraging on mosses and lichens. The majority of reindeer in Sweden and northern Norway are semi-domesticated and owned by the Samer (Lapps). Some of their animals summer in the mountains and move to warmer forest areas in winter. The animals of Finnmarksvidda journey from this plateau to the coast and offshore islands to avoid the insects of the short summer. These flocks may have been seriously endangered by radio-active fallout from the Russian nuclear disaster in 1986.

Musk oxen were introduced into the Dovre National Park in central Norway more than 20 years ago. They appear to be thriving in their apparently harsh environment, although total numbers are not large. They are great wanderers and offshoot herds have developed in Rondane and Femundsmarka, also in Swedish Harjedalen province. These high Arctic animals have amazing insulation and appear to be indifferent to even the coldest weather. Although shy and normally unaggressive, they can be dangerous if approached too close, especially cows with young. Apparent clumsiness is misleading as they can run amazingly fast uphill and over rocky ground. Fatalities have occurred - photographers please note.

Brown bear, wolf, wolverine and lynx are all known in the wilder mountain and forest areas. All are officially protected. The wolf is virtually gone, but fresh animals periodically migrate from Russia and Finland into Norway. Rabies is prevalent in Russian and possibly Finnish wolves and because of this real danger most immigrant animals are shot. The Samer (Lapps) have a long established fear and dislike of all large predators and shoot any wolves. Elsewhere there is a growing sympathy for the wolf as an endangered species; the national Swedish conservation organisation (SNF) is fighting a last ditch campaign to save the remainder.

The brown bear still survives in modest numbers and can be found in forested valleys in some mountain areas. Their strongholds are in the deeper forests, especially the more southerly Norway/Sweden border areas. Wolverine numbers are not large, but it is a solitary and wily animal. Winter is the best time to catch a glimpse of one of these elusive animals which seem to love high, wild mountains. Their strange tracks can often be seen at considerable heights.

Lynx have been increasing in northern and central forest areas of Sweden, geared to an increasing population of roe deer. They are not confined to the forests and in winter their tracks can be found above the tree line. Quite recently there have been reports of the population being affected by disease. Red fox and Arctic fox are probably the most likely mammals to be seen in the mountains, even though the latter is localised. Both have suffered from a similar disease to that damaging the lynx population.

Of importance among the smaller mammals are lemming and short-tailed vole. The former are legendary for their swarming and apparently suicidal behaviour, caused by excessive local population growth outstripping available food supplies. The swarming, migrating mass - a rare spectacle in itself - is heightened by the numerous animal and bird predators following its passage. To a lesser extent the short-tailed vole has similar population cycles and movements.

Birdlife in Scandinavia is rich and varied, particularly in Sweden, but
in mountain areas it is rather poorer though still with considerable interest. Birds of prey are well represented with a significant population
of Europe's white-tailed eagle and gyrfalcon. Rough legged and common buzzard are found fairly high, and the honey buzzard at lower
altitudes, along with the aggressive goshawk. The spectacular snowy
owl is a plateau and tundra bird whose numbers are linked to the cycle
of lemming and voles, as also is the flamboyant long-tailed skua.

Forested lower levels of many mountain areas contain good numbers of
birds including a wide range of woodpeckers and owls, most prominent
in Sweden; great gray owl, ural owl, hawk owl, even pygmy owl;
black, green, gray-headed, white backed and 3 toed woodpeckers
as well as more common species. The friendly and colourful Siberian
jay has been a visitor to many camps, even in the winter.

The high open plateaux (viddas) and tundra is the breeding ground in
summer for large numbers of wading birds. Their beautiful colours, eg
dotterel, red necked phalarope, along with their haunting calls and
song (greenshank, golden plover), add greatly to the wilderness atmosphere of the northern mountains.

THE SAMER (or Lapps)

Almost everyone has heard of Lappland, a name that conjures up visions
of a vast northern wilderness with forests, mountains, reindeer and a
traditional pastoral people. Putting a geographical boundary on Lappland is not easy because the overall location encompasses parts of Norway, Sweden, Finland and even Russia. It seems logical to call the
people of Lappland either Lapplanders or Lapps; but unfortunately the
latter name has a slightly derogatory meaning. They call themselves
Samer, or Sami, and this is worth remembering.

There are approximately 20,000 Samer in Norway and about 15,000 in
Sweden, some of whom still try to live close to their traditional and
pastoral way of life. It is important that all mountain users know and
understand something of their traditions and lifestyle in order to avoid
clashes of interest.

The Samer have been responsible for the naming of most features in the
northern mountain areas; not just in the region known as Lappland, but
as far S as Härjedalen in Sweden and Femundsmarka in Norway. Their
language and culture are reflected in the colourful and descriptive
names given to many mountain features; some examples may illustrate
this. "Äppartjåkko" mountain means "The ghost of the murdered child".
"Kvikjokk" means "The rapidly flowing river". "Vuojatätno" means
"The river with the swimming-over place" and probably describes a

reindeer migration point, now disused. Some mountain names are almost unbelievably long and difficult to pronounce - Kaskasanjunjetjåkka in the Kebnekaise group.

Their culture and language differs enormously from that of other Scandinavians. In recent years there have been a number of conflicts of interest. Long legal battles have been fought between the Samer and the Swedish crown over the question of ownership of vast areas. The Samer have lost and are naturally unhappy at the outcome. Where the large mountain huts have been constructed in Sweden, the Samer claim that more people are encouraged to wander in the mountains with increased potential disturbance to reindeer. Faceless authorities, in particular the electricity industry, with apparently unlimited powers have built dams and access roads, flooding valleys used traditionally for the movement of reindeer. In some cases the Samer have been forced entirely to abandon their lifestyle and now live in permanent settlements. The final insult to some has been refusal of electricity supplies to settlements on the grounds of uneconomical connexion.

Lappland is important for the diminishing numbers of predator mammals, all of whom predate reindeer to some extent. Conservationists attempting to preserve these species are soon at odds with a people who still see these animals as a threat to their livelihood.

Since the nuclear disaster at Chernobyl in 1986 the Samer face a new threat, perhaps their worst ever. Lichens have been shown to accumulate very high concentrations of radiation. This has rapidly been passed on to the reindeer, whose meat has proved to be contaminated to a level many times the safe limits. Sale and use of reindeer meat is of paramount importance to the Samer and at the annual slaughter of animals more than 90% have been condemned as unfit for consumption. How many years this may last and the scale of financial and possibly cultural disaster that may follow is not yet known.

It is hoped that visitors in summer and winter will behave in a manner which respects the fact that many Samer still depend on these mountain areas for their livelihood. Please don't disturb the reindeer deliberately or accidentally, for example by close-up photography. Nor damage or misuse the kåta (simple dwellings), even if they are apparently not in use. The Samer recognise 8 distinct seasons in the year. Please leave the fish and berries for those that live there all the seasons.

A. SOUTHERN HIGHLANDS

Rogaland/Setesdal

A VERY large area of upland, some 4500 sq. ml, or put another way, 5 times the size of the Lake District National Park. It is an interesting and varied landscape with a combination of hills and mountains, deep valleys, rivers, lakes, fjords and even small remnant glaciers of the ice cap type. The highest ground is in the N and rises to over 1600m.

In recent years the whole area has been the subject of some huge hydro-electric power developments. The proliferation of power lines, access roads and dams, some of which have flooded vast areas, has spoiled the character of the landscape. Being situated in the SW the climate is greatly influenced by Atlantic depressions. In general there is high rainfall in summer and heavy snowfall in winter, though sometimes with long spells of fine weather.

The northern districts are the home of several thousand wild reindeer; there is also a good variety of birds and flowers. Many walking tourers carry fishing rods and a licence is easy to obtain locally. Fishing has declined in recent years - reputedly through the effects of acid rain.

For the purposes of mountain touring, in summer and winter, there is great scope and variety. The 3 local touring associations have laid out a fine network of walking trails and constructed more than 40 mountain huts, producing one of the best area systems within Norway. Outside Norway the area is not well known for its rock climbing and probably for this reason receives few visits from foreign climbers. There are a lot of routes both in the Lysefjord area and on the huge granite slabs of Setesdalen; information is scanty and is best obtained from the local associations.

The area boundaries are: In the N the E76 road separates the area from the Hardanger plateau; in the W the sea and lower ground; in the E the upland finishes along a rough line joining the inland Byglandsfjord in the southern part, through Fyresvatn to meet the E76 in the northern part; in the S the border is not well defined - it approximates with the E-W route 9.

APPROACHES

Most districts are best approached from Stavanger or Kristiansand; Bergen is a good alternative for northern districts. It is possible to travel from Oslo by rail, via Kristiansand, as far as Stavanger. With an area as large as this one there are many possible approaches; those listed below are the easiest and most direct.

Local boats serve much of the western flank, departing from Stavanger or Bergen; some are car ferries. Local buses from Kristiansand are very useful; from Stavanger or Bergen they are not so frequent/direct. Useful information is to be found in the annual leaflet "Tourist Timetables" published by the Norwegian Tourist Office, but many local services are omitted.

Using your own transport (access problems in winter) from Kristiansand go N on route 12 through Evje, past Byglandsfjord and eventually along the Setesdal. This takes you past a number of good starting points for tours; to Hovden is 219 km. and to Haukeligrend 248 km. For the S and W districts follow route 12 to Kjetså, 58 km; turn W along route 9 to Sveindal, 19 km. (for Åseral, Ljoslandhytta and others); continue to Tonstad in a further 80 km. and take route 468 N to Ådneram and other points.

From Stavanger follow the E18 through Ålgård for about 26 km; turn NE along route 45 into the Sirdal where it becomes route 468. A small road leading N to Ådneram gives access to the southern district.

From Bergen leave by the E68 going E as far as Kvanndal (130 km.); ferry to Utne and S to Odda; or alternative ferry to Kinsarvik and then S on route 47 to Odda, this latter being the better road (41 km.); continue to junction with the E76 which is followed SE past several starting points, eventually to Haukeligrend in a further 105 km. from Odda.

BASES

As an area primarily used for mountain touring on foot or ski, there are no ideal bases for overall exploration. Rather a large number of possible starting points, adopted according to which of many possible route combinations are used. Food and other supplies are available at most of the self-service and some of the fully serviced huts. There are no towns within the boundaries of the area. The choice is one between high prices on the spot or carrying large pack loads.

MAPS

CAP sh.1 325M Southern Norway, shows the entire region, all approaches and minor roads clearly; includes Bergen, Stavanger, Kristiansand and Oslo. Much of the area is covered by the new type SK 50M survey. A few sheets are still only available in the old series; these are indicated (O) and are due to be replaced in 1988. Missing hydro-electric developments is a serious problem with many of these maps.

1212 I	Høle	1413 I	Urdenosi
1312 I	Øvre Sirdal	1413 II	Valle
1312 IV	Frafjord	1413 III	Rjuven
1313 I	Blåfjell	1413 IV	Botsvatn
1313 II	Lysekammen	1414 II	Saesvatn
1313 III	Lyngsvatnet (O)	1414 III	Breive
1313 IV	Sand (O)	1414 IV	Haukelisaeter
1314 I	Røldal	1512 I	Gjøvdal
1314 II	Suldalsvatnet	1512 IV	Bygland
1314 III	Sauda (O)	1513 III	Grossae
1412 I	Austad	1513 IV	Dalen
1412 IV	Kvifjorden	1514 III	Vinje

2 special tourist maps at 80M cover much of the area and are more modern, issued in 1984 and 1985.

sh 31 Sirdal-Setesdalsheiane   sh 97 Suldal-Setesdalsheiane

HUTS and other accommodation

Huts are owned or controlled by 3 separate regional associations, all affiliated to DNT. During the normal summer season all huts are unlocked in Rogalandheiene and Setedalsheiene. Unstaffed huts in Austheiene are locked at all times; key from AOT office. Hut lists, up to date opening times, prices and special key enquiries out of normal seasons should be addressed directly to the appropriate association.

1. Stavanger Tourist Association (ST), Turistpaviljongen,
   4000 Stavanger   (for Rogalandsheiene)
2. Kristiansand & Oppland Tourist Association (KOT), Rådhusgatan 5,
   4600 Kristiansand (for Setedalsheiene)
3. Arendal & Oppland Tourist Association (AOT) (for Austheiene).

Rogalandsheiene

Staffed huts:	beds	Map No.	4-fig. ref.
Breiborg Turisthytte	32	1314 III	63-23
Haukeliseter Fjellstue	110	1414 IV	98-33
Ådneram Turisthytte	41	1313 II	81-44
Prekestolhytta	56	1212 I	35-42
Stranddalshytta	22	1313 I	70-91

Self-service huts:	beds	Map No.	4-fig. ref.
Bleskestadmoen	14	1414 III	86-11
Eidavatn	12	1313 I	71-72
Melandsgrønahei	12	1313 III	60-70
Holmevasshytta	14	1413 III	94-20
Hovatn	16	1413 IV	89-82
Kringlevatn	16	1413 III	88-68
Krossvatn	16	1313 I	81-93
Kvilldal Turiststasjon	12	1314 II	66-99
Litle Aurådal	8	1313 II	77-62
Mostøl	15	1314 II	78-05
Nilsebu	28	1313 II	67-63
Taumevatn	12	1413 III	84-53
Storsteinen	16	1313 I	80-73

Unstaffed huts:

	beds	Map No.	4-fig. ref.
Lysebotn Turiststasjon	20	1313 II	65-48
Kvanndalen	4	1414 III	87-19
Viglesdalshytta	8	1313 III	54-60
Grautheller	8	1313 II	79-55
Grasdalshytta	11	1313 II	64-68
Sandsahytta	42	1313 IV	63-91

Setedalsheiene

Staffed huts:

	beds	Map No.	4-fig. ref.
Bjørnevannshytta	32	1413 I	16-79
Ljoslandshytta	59	1412 I	04-17
Gaukheihytta	41	1412 IV	02-32
Hovdehytta	92	1414 II	07-03

Self-service huts:

	beds	Map No.	4-fig. ref.
Øyuvsbu	40	1413 III	98-44
Bossbu	34	1413 III	02-61
Sloaroshytta	21	1414 III	01-13
Svartenuthytta	24	1413 III	99-56

Unstaffed huts:

	beds	Map No.	4-fig. ref.
Stakkedalen	10	1412 I	11-36
Stavskarhytta	10	1413 II	08-63

Austheiene Self-service

	beds	Map No.	4-fig. ref.
Berdalsbu	12	1413 I	15-90

Self-service huts:	beds	Map No.	4-fig. ref.
Granbustøyl	8	1513 III	39-41
Hovstøyl	12	1513 IV	29-69
Nutevasshytta	14	1513 III	39-41
Nystøyl	8	1513 III	27-59
Tjørnbrotbu	14	1414 II	16-01
Unstaffed huts:			
Gamasbø	4	1413 II	23-67
Gjuvasstøyl	4	1413 I	24-70
Torsdalsbu	3	1513 III	29-63
Vindilhytta	30	1512 I	48-36

Youth Hostels at Nesflaten, Bykle and Dalen. For full details see YH handbook.

WALKING TOURS

With such a large number of huts and marked paths available, possible touring combinations are too numerous to list here. For those who wish to backpack and/or find their own unmarked routes the possibilities are even greater. Some suggested tours are as follows.

1. Haukeliseter to Suldal (about 5 days)
Haukeliseter – Holmevasshytta – Bleskestadmoen – Mostøl – Stranddal-shytta – Kvilldal.

2. Åseral to Bykle (about 5 days)
Ljosandshytta – Gaukheihytta – Øyuvsbu – Svartenuthytta – Bossbu – Bykle.

3. Hovden to Gjøvdal (about 8 days)
Hovden – Tjørnbrotbu – Berdalsbu – Bjørnevasshytta – Hovstøyl – Nyst-øyl – Nutevasshytta – Granbustøyl – Vindilhytta.

4. Ådneram to Kvilldal (about 7 days)
Ådneram – Taumevatn – Kringlevatn – Storsteinen – Hovatn – Krossvatn – Stranddalshytta – Kvilldal.

Further suggestions may be obtained from DNT or the local mountain touring associations, but part of the pleasure of long distance touring is planning your own routes.

Even longer trips can be made by linking those in this area with those of the Hardanger area to the N.

Hardangervidda locality

THE HUGE upland plateau of Hardangervidda has an associated ice-cap in the NW - Hardanger Jøkulen, and for convenience the nearby glacier of Folgefonn (W of Sørfjorden) may also be included, although it is not part of the vidda proper. The total overall area exceeds 7500 sq.km. (3000 sq.ml.) and the 2 ice-caps contribute some 260 sq.km. (140 sq. ml.). Since 1981 an area of 3430 sq.km. has been designated Hardangervidda National Park.

Hardangervidda is well known for its hut to hut touring, either on foot or by ski. An elaborate network of marked paths and huts are maintained mainly by DNT. The vidda proper forms an unbroken unit, uncrossed by any major valley and has an unusually remote and peaceful atmosphere. The central districts are gently undulating with most hills rising only a little above the general landscape. There are many lakes and marshes and the vidda gives relaxing rather than spectacular touring, with flowers, birds, mammals and fishing as additional attractions. On its E and W edges the plateau drops away extremely steeply, with some of the highest and most impressive gorges and waterfalls in Scandinavia; some falls exceed 200m. in height.

The 2 ice-caps give added variety to the scenery and Hardanger Jøkulen at 1862m. marks the highest point in the northern area. There is a growing interest in glacier crossings and snow/ice ascents in Norway and this ice-cap is particularly popular. Folgefonn gl. is situated between 2 sea fjords in a wild and lovely setting. It is less used, though there is good skiing plus rock and ice climbing possibilities; details may be available from Bergen Turlag.

Being situated in the far W of Norway the area is strongly influenced by Atlantic depressions. The relatively smooth surface of the vidda is noted for its ferocious winds, particularly early to mid-winter. It is a high rainfall and snowfall area, hence the ice-caps.

Hardangervidda is also notable for its wildlife, with a matchless birdlife, an attractive flora and huge herds of wild reindeer. In recent times up to 40,000, the numbers are now reduced to preserve the area from overgrazing. Other mammals include the most southerly arctic foxes in Scandinavia. Southerly ranging bird species include snowy owl, long-tailed skua, Lappland bunting and shore lark, all normally found much further N.

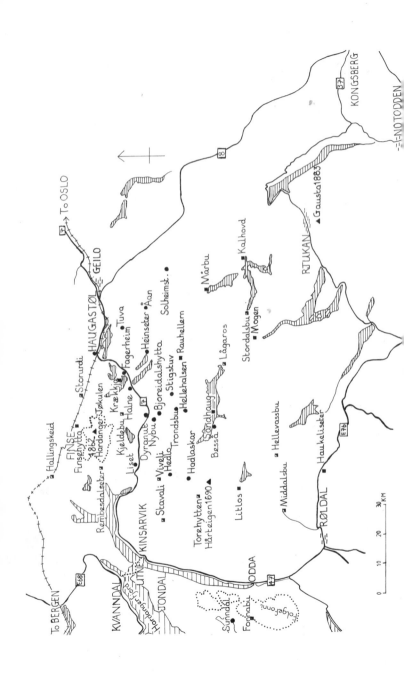

The boundary in the N is marked by the railway from Bergen to Oslo, running through Finse (the highest station in Scandinavia); in the W, Hardangerfjord provides a natural border; in the E the boundary is less well defined, being the low country roughly following the N-S route 8; in the S the E76 road separates this area from Rogaland/Setesdal.

APPROACHES

Bergen is the most convenient starting point. Access from Oslo by rail is good for the northern parts and Hardanger Jøkulen. The Bergen railway provides good, regular all year round access with several trains daily. There are bus services from Bergen to Kvanndal, followed by a ferry to Kinsarvik; then bus services E along route 7 with many possible starting points for the vidda. This route is closed in winter. Alternatively, bus services S from Kinsarvik are useful for Folgefonn and the western sections of the vidda. From Oslo all year round buses serve the eastern areas of the vidda, via Kongsberg or Notodden.

Using your own transport the easiest approach is from Bergen via the E68 to Kvanndal (130 km.); ferry to Kinsarvik and S to Odda along route 47 (41 km.), passing a number of western flank starting points; continue to junction with E76 and along to Haukeliseter for the S flanks of the vidda. Folgefonn can be approached the same way, but take the ferry to Utne only and follow a small road S under the steep E side of the ice-cap.

For the N side of the vidda and for the Jøkulen continue from Kinsarvik E along route 7 (now much improved), passing numerous excellent starting points en route. Haugastøl at the E edge is 97 km. from Kinsarvik.

The E flank and gorges of the vidda are best approached from Oslo, although it is possible to continue along the previous route 7 to Geilo; then go S on route 8 (with some starting points); finally head W on small roads to Rjukan and other offshoot roads and starting points, a further 112 km. Alternatively go N on route 8 and towards Geilo.

BASES

Because this area is used mainly for hut to hut or camping tours, there are no bases ideal for exploring the vidda, or even a major part of it. Many starting points are possible; some have been indicated above and others are listed under suggestions for touring. For the ice-caps it is practical to use a base for a thorough exploration. Odda at the head of Sørfjorden is possible for Folgefonn; a town of over 7000 people it has food shops and other facilities. Finse is convenient for Hardanger Jøkulen; access by rail (no road). It is a tourist complex and village with a useful shop.

Provisions are available for sale at many of the self-service huts and meals at the fully serviced huts. Prices are high, so as usual the choice is between economical camping with a big pack or expensive convenience and ease.

MAPS

CAP sh.1 325M Southern Norway and sh.2 Central Norway I show the area and approaches well. Sh.2 does not show all the southern approaches, but is useful for those wishing to go further N too. SK produce a special tourist map Hardangervidda at 200M scale. For detailed navigation most of the area is now covered by the new SK 50M maps; only the Folgefonn district remains in the old series (O).

1315 I	Ullensvang	1416 II	Hardangerjøkulen
1315 II	Ringedalsvatnet	1416 III	Myrdal
1315 III	Odda (O)	1514 I	Frøystoul
1315 IV	Jondal (O)	1514 IV	Møsstrand
1316 II	Ulvik	1515 I	Skurdalen
1414 I	Songevatnet	1515 II	Kalhovd
1414 IV	Haukeliseter	1515 III	Lågaros
1415 I	Bjoreio	1515 IV	Hein
1415 II	Nordmannslågen	1614 IV	Rjukan
1415 III	Hårteigen	1615 IV	Uvdal
1415 IV	Eidfjord		

HUTS and other accommodation

Huts are controlled by DNT and 3 regional mountain touring associations. In addition there are privately owned huts comprising part of the network. Most self-service huts are fitted with standard DNT locks, but it is best to enquire beforehand from the appropriate association, who can also supply up to date prices and other hut details. 1. Bergen Turlag (BT), C. Sundsgaten 3, 5000 Bergen. 2. Drammen & Opplands Turistforening (DOT), 3000 Drammen. 3. Skien-Telemarks Turistforening (STT), 3700 Skien.

Staffed huts:	beds	Map No.	4 fig. ref.
Finsehytta (DNT)	114	1416 II	18–19
Kalhovd Turisthytte (STT)	70	1515 II	65–59
Kraekkjahytta (DNT)	76	1415 I	29–02
Litlos (DNT)	52	1415 III	96–63
Mogen Turisthytte (STT)	48	1515 III	38–54
Mårbu	35	1515 II	54–72
Rauhellern (DOT)	50	1515 IV	36–80
Sandhaug (DNT)	82	1415 II	15–73

Private staffed huts (normally completely locked out of season):

Besså Turisthytte	30	1415 II	11-72
Bjoreidalshytta	40	1415 I	19-89
Dyranut Fjellstue	20	1415 I	17-93
Dyranut Turisthytte	55	1415 I	17-93
Fagerheim Fjellstue	90	1515 IV	34-01
Hadlaskar Turisthytte	20	1415 IV	98-80
Halne Fjellstove	30	1415 I	27-98
Hein Seter	15	1515 IV	41-91
Hedlo	50	1415 IV	98-87
Hellehalsen Turisthytte	20	1415 I	19-81
Hol Gard	10	1415 IV	04-99
Liset Pensjonat	40	1415 IV	05-99
Nybu	15	1415 I	17-90
Solheimstulen	43	1515 I	63-85
Stigstuv Turisthytte	36	1415 I	25-85
Trondsbu Turisthytte	15	1415 I	20-85
Tuva Seter	20	1515 IV	47-01
Viveli Turistasjon	25	1415 IV	97-91
Åan Turisthytte	23	1515 I	54-94

Self-service huts:

Fonnabu (BT)	16	1315 III	52-62
Hellevassbu (DNT)	26	1414 IV	00-51
Kjeldebu (DNT)	40	1415 I	13-01
Lågaros (DNT)	32	1515 III	33-66
Middalsbu (DNT)	8	1414 IV	87-48
Rembesdalseter (DNT)	18	1416 III	05-12
Stavalihytta (BT)	30	1315 I	83-88
Stordalsbu (DNT)	12	1515 II	50-58
Storurdi (BT)	24	1416 II	25-14
Torehytten (DNT)	18	1415 III	91-76
Viveli Fjellstove (BT)	65	1415 IV	97-91

Unstaffed huts:

Breidablikk (BT)	4	1315 III	52-64
Dalamot Seter (BT)	4	1315 I	87-97

Youth hostels at Geilo, Odda, Rjukan and Uvdal. For full details see YH handbook.

WALKING TOURS

There are about 1200 km. of marked trails in Hardangervidda alone, linking virtually 40 huts. Scope for the wanderer and backpacker is even greater. A few suggested tours are as follows.

1. **Finse to Haukeliseter** (about 8 days)
Finse – Kraekkja – Kjeldebu – Liset – Hedlo – Sandhaug – Litlos – Hellevassbu – Haukeliseter. Possible extension further S into the Rogaland/Setesdal area.

2. **Rjukan to Kinsarvik** (about 7 days)
Rjukan – Mogen – Lågaros – Sandhaug – Litlos – Torehytten – Stavali – Kinsarvik.
This route can include an ascent of Hårteigen (1690m.), the highest point of the central vidda and a distinctly rocky summit. Total ascent from the Litlos – Torehytten trail is about 200m. through the only line of weakness; an interesting and steep scramble protected by fixed ropes.

3. **Roldal to Kinsarvik** (about 5 days)
Roldal – Middalsby – Litlos – Sandhaug – Bjoreidal – Kinsarvik.

4. **Around the Hardanger Jøkulen** (about 4 days)
Finse – Kjeldebu – Rembesdalseter – Finse.

MOUNTAIN ASCENTS

Hårteigen
See above. The steep summit wall of gneiss possibly has potential.

Hardanger Jøkulen
Several snow/ice ascents are possible using the gl. tongues and numerous snow gullies. Crevasses are normally present and should not be underestimated. Some potential for rock routes.

Folgefonn
Usually crossed along the E – W axis. Odda, Rosendal, Jondal and Sunndal are starting points. There is also a ski tour along the 37km. N – S axis, starting at Rosendal and finishing at Jondal. The long and steep eastern wall has apparently some potential rock and ice routes; details are scarce.

Hårteigen – Hardangervidda

B. CENTRAL MOUNTAINS

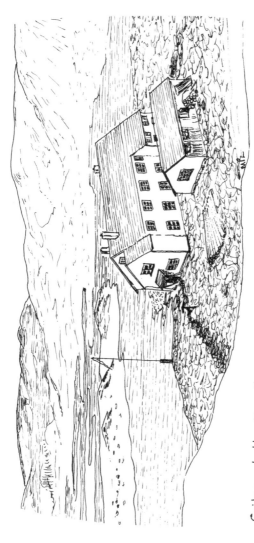

Gøitorygghytta (Area 3)

Hallingskarvet & Fillefjell

THESE are a series of individually recognisable but interconnected ranges linking the huge Southern Region plateaux with the higher summits of the Jotunheimen area. The mountains are divided on the E by several deep and wide valleys, in particular those of Hemsedal and Sudndalen. Several remnant ice-caps exist in the S and W districts. The highest summit of Hallingskarvet is Folarskardnuten, 1933m; in the Fillefjell, Jukleeggi reaches 1920m.

A good area for long distance walking or ski-touring, there are also summits suitable for ascents and some fine climbing on local crags. The pattern of transverse valleys and ridges produces great scenic beauty with some especially attractive waterfalls dropping into the heavily forested valleys. The forests hold roe deer and elk and must be one of the most southerly locations for siberian jay. Other notable birds include gyr falcon, great snipe and dotterel. On the higher open fjells the flora is diverse. Being further E than Hardangervidda, the climate is generally drier. The Hallingskarvet is still prone to westerly storms, but some of the eastern valleys almost have a rain shadow climate.

The boundaries are, in the N, the E68 from Lake Vangsmjøsi to Lake Tyin, then route 53 to Sognefjord; in the W the railway from Myrdal to Flåm, then the SE arms of Sognefjord. The E side is more difficult to define - roughly a line drawn N - S between Gol and Lake Vangsmjøsi; in the S the Bergen railway line.

APPROACHES

From Bergen modern express boat (hyrdofoil) service goes up to the head of Sognefjord in only 6h. (no vehicles). Some services are all year round; among others Aurland, Laerdalsøyri and Årdalstangen can be reached thus. The rail link is convenient and even quicker; some stations - Myrdal, Finse and Haugastøl - offer suitable starting points (3h. to Finse). Further on from Hol and Gol bus links go into E Hallingskarvet and the subsidiary Reineskarvet range.

From Oslo the railway is equally convenient; similarly for the E side (about 4h. to Gol). An alternative line goes to Fagernes, followed by bus along the E68 to Lake Vangsmjøsi. At peak holiday times there are special coaches direct from Oslo to Geilo and Fagernes.

Using your own transport from Bergen follow the E68 to Kvanndal (130 km.), ferry to Kinsarvik, then route 7 across Hardangervidda to Gol (171 km.), hence NW on route 52 through Hemsedal for the Fillefjell. Alternatively, only as far as Hol (132 km.), then NW on route 288 through Sudndalen for E Hallingskarvet.

From Oslo take the E68 to Hønefoss, then route 7 to Gol (199 km.) or on to Hol (238 km.). Alternatively the E68 to Fagernes (191 km.).

BASES

In this primarily touring area there are few bases with suitable facilities for a prolonged stay. Finse can be used for ascents in the Hallingskarvet combined with routes on the Hardanger Jøkulen (Area 2).

Hemsedal is a good town base with all facilities; bank, food shops, garages, etc. Good rock climbing too, details of which the residents are reluctant to reveal. Try the shop: Skandinavisk Høyfjellsutstyr.

MAPS

CAP 325M sh.2 Central Norway I shows the area and approaches well. SK 50M survey maps are all new series.

1416 I	Aurlandsdalen	1516 III	Hallingskarvet
1416 II	Hardangerjøkulen	1516 IV	Djup
1416 III	Myrdal	1517 II	Øye
1416 IV	Aurland	1517 III	Borgund
1417 II	Laerdalsøyri	1616 III	Ål
1516 I	Gyrinosvatnet	1616 IV	Hemsedal
1516 II	Geilo	1617 III	Vangsmjøsi

HUTS and other accommodation

All huts in this area are either DNT contolled or privately owned. All self-service DNT huts are fitted with standard locks.

Staffed huts:	beds	Map No.	4-fig. ref.
Finsehytta	114	1416 II	18-19
Geiterygghytta	82	1416 II	23-30
Iungsdalshytta	32	1516 IV	42-42
Self-service huts:			
Bjordalsbu	22	1516 IV	45-55
Kljåen	7	1517 II	62-66
Kongshelleren	12	1416 I	29-38
Slettningsbu	14	1517 II	53-90
Sulebu	16	1517 II	56-78

Private (staffed) huts:	beds	Map No.	4-fig. ref.
Raggsteindalshytta	80	1516 III	36-26
Steinbergdalshytta	30	1416 I	22-39
Stonndalen Turisthytte	30	1416 I	10-45
Øvstebø Fjellstova	60	1416 I	18-44
Øvstebø Turisthytte	50	1416 I	18-44

YH at Borlaug, Geilo and Laerdal. Øvstebø Fjellstova also serves as a hostel.

WALKING TOURS

There are fewer marked trails compared with Areas 1 and 2. Suggested routes are as follows.

1. Finse to Aurland (about 5 days)
Finse - Geiterygghytta - Steinbergdalshytta - Øvstebø - Aurland.

2. Haugastøl to Nystova (about 6 days)
Haugastøl - Raggsteindalshytta - lungsdalshytta - Bjordalsbu - Breistølen - Sulebu - Nystova (on E68). Alternatively from Bjordalsbu to Kljåen. From here, optional ascent of Jukleeggi (1920m.), highest summit in the Fillefjell. Round trip, 5h. Continue, Kljåen - Sulebu.

3. Finse to Slettningsbu (about 8-9 days)
A classic high level route to the Jotunheimen. Finse - Geiterygghytta - Kongshelleren - lungsdalshytta - Bjordalsbu - Breistølen - Sulebu - Slettningsbu. This route can be easily continued into any district of the Jotunheimen mountains.

MOUNTAIN ASCENTS

Hallingskarvet main ridge is several km. long and presents rocky walls on both N and S faces. The S is particularly steep and in places 300m. high. This ridge is broken by 2 important passes used by tourers, which also provide easy access to the summit plateaux.

Folarskardnuten 1933m.
Easy scramble and walk. From Haugastøl or Raggsteindalshytta go up to the pass of Folarskardet, about 5h. from former, 4h.+ from the latter. Scramble up easy sound rock to W onto broad, stony plateau summit, 1h.

Other separate summits worthy of ascent for viewpoints are Kyrkjedørsnuten (1790m.) and Storesåta (1849m.). On closer inspection the main walls are not very promising - very broken and often loose. There are possibilities, but virtually no record of ascents. Tvergasteinskarv S face was ascended in 1937 by A Naess. Believed to be wall above the tarn of that name - no other details are available. Rock climbing has been done on the crags above the Storurdi hut; details may be available from Bergen Turlag.

Around Hemsedal there are a number of crags with climbs up to 375m. of all grades. The rock is generally compact and sound, with some very fine routes. Descriptions and gradings have so far been withheld by local climbers to "protect" the area. This kind of situation prevails in many parts of the Scandinavian mountains.

honey buzzard

Jotunheimen

WITHOUT doubt the most famous mountain area in Scandinavia and the legendary "Home of the Giants". Norwegian mountaineering was born here as a result of explorations begun in 1872 by the Yorkshireman William Cecil Slingsby. He made 15 expeditions to Norway up to the First World War. His first ascent, the final part solo, of Store Skagastølstind in 1876 remains one of the most celebrated feats in the annals of a mountain range where the Norwegians themselves have subsequently prevailed.

Although 3900 sq. km. in extent, it is not particularly large compared with some, but it holds a greater concentration of high mountains than any other area. The 2 highest summits in Scandinavia, Galdhøpiggen (2469m.) and Glittertind (2464m.) - once considered equal but whose ice-cap is now lower, are both found here, plus more than 200 summits over 1900m.

The Jotunheimen is outstandingly beautiful and varigated with dramatic differences between the rolling fjells of the E and the jagged ridges and soaring walls of the W. The 2 great lakes of Bygdin and Gjende have long been celebrated in legend and the highest waterfall (275m.) in Norway, Vettisfossen, is found in the W of the area.

The great majority of peaks are composed of gabbro. This normally hard and resistant rock has encouraged the formation of spectacular mountain scenery, particularly in the W districts of Hurrungane and Smørstabb. Weathering and climatic conditions are severe so that the quality of the rock is not always good. These same factors have also produced extensive boulderfields, often unstable and sometimes set at very steep angles. There is often an unexpectedly heavy growth of lichen on rock and boulders. When wet this can be dangerously slippery and can put a climb up a couple of grades.

The earliest visitors to the Jotunheimen were reindeer hunters and botanists. Today the wild reindeer have disappeared, although semi-tame herds can be found in most districts. Botanically the area is still exceptional with many species of Arctic and even Alpine flowers. Birds and mammals are relatively thin; the rough-legged buzzard is seen in some years and the rare gyr falcon breeds in at least one district. Today the most numerous visitors are summer walkers touring from hut to hut or

57

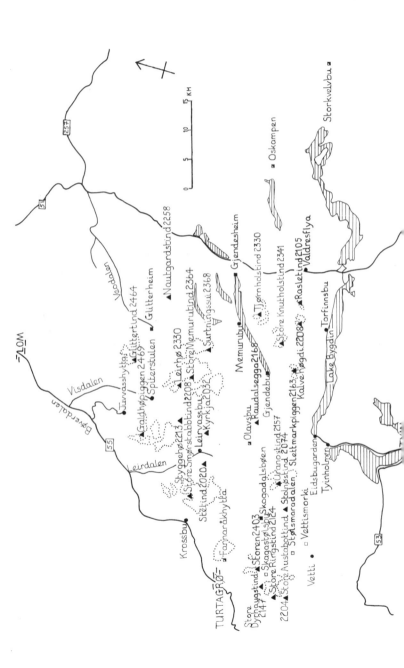

backpacking; the latter are probably outnumbered 20 : 1 by the former. A tiny minority come to ascend the mountains - walking, scrambling or climbing. Consequently it is still unusual to meet another party on the same ascent. In winter few huts are open, except for the short, busy Easter period. Ski-touring here is more serious than in other areas, with increased avalanche danger, and out of the Easter period difficulties with accommodation.

The climatic differences E to W are almost as dramatic as the scenery. The Hurrungane group in particular is notorious for its cloud, lying as it does at the head of Sognefjord. This W district is a high precipitation area and the old Met. station (now a DNT hut) on the summit of Fannaråki (2068m.) has produced some awesome statistics. This location averages 319 days below freezing; 200 days with significant precipitation; 223 days with more than 85% cloud cover. Only a few km. E the important base of Spiterstulen enjoys much improved weather conditions, while a few km. further the valley town of Lom boasts a "rain-shadow" climate. For the area as a whole W winds normally bring poor weather, winds from the E dry weather.

Boundaries: in the N the deep valley of Ottadalen and route 15, then route 55; in the W it is roughly confined by the Sognefjord and the Jostedal ice-cap with its satellites; in the E the N-S route 51 forms an effective boundary to the highest summits, but there is a long SE extension of fjells stretching almost to Gudbrandsdalen; in the S the Fillefjell mountains.

APPROACHES

From Oslo by rail to Otta; bus to Lom, on through Bøverdalen and Leirdalen for access to N districts. Or by rail/bus to Fagernes, then bus to Bygdin and Gjendesheim for E districts; or W from Fagernes by bus to Tyin and Eidsbugarden for S districts.
    From Bergen by boat up Sognefjord to Leikanger with bus to Turtagro for the W; alternatively continue to Årdalstangen (about 6½ h. from Bergen), then bus to Tyin, etc. for S.

Using your own transport from Oslo go N on E6 to Otta (308 km.); route 15 to Lom (64km.); finally route 55 to various minor roads (often with heavy tolls) to bases such as Spiterstulen and Leirvassbu in the N. For E districts use E68 to Fagernes (191 km.); route 51 to Bygdin and Gjendesheim (52 or 74km.); for S district continue on E68 to Hugostua (75km.), then route 53 for Tyin.
    From Bergen follow E68 to Trengereid (41 km.), then route 13 to Vangsnes (164km.), ferry to Hella followed by route 5 to Sogndal (37 km.) and finally route 55 to Turtagrø (76km.) for W. Or from Sogndal continue on route 5 to Kaupanger (11 km.), ferry to Revsnes and route E68

to Tyin (90 km.) for S districts. By the E and S final approaches, a boat along lakes Bygdin and Gjende gives central access.

BASES

For tourers there are numerous possible starting points. See routes and approaches outlined below. For walking and climbing ascents there are a few suitable bases, mainly with good accommodation facilities, sometimes with food supplies and usually accessible by road. To get the best out of a number of mountains or groups it will be necessary to be self-sufficient and use a camping base. The Jotunheimen can be divided into workable districts. The NTK has named 9 separate districts, but for our purposes 4 will suffice.

1. W district; to include the mountain groups Hurrungane and Smørstabb – the best overall climbing district. The traditional base is Turtagrø and its hotel, although it is best to camp in Skagastølsdalen or Ringsdalen. For the Smørstabb group, the Krossbu/Sognefjellhytta or Leirvassbu huts are well placed alternatives to camping.

2. South-Central district; to include the Bygdin-Gjende ranges and the SW Utla-Tyin mountain group. Gjendebu has some provisions for sale; Olavsbu has provisions; Torfinnsbu, Tyinholmen or Eidsbugarden are fully serviced huts/hotels.

3. North-Central district; to include the Galdhøpiggen, Glittertind and Memurubu mountain groups. Spiterstulen and Leirvassbu are comfortable bases but have little for the self-catering visitor, similarly with Glitterheim and Gjendesheim. Olavsbu has provisions.

4. E and SE district; mainly the fjells lying E of route 51 and to S of Lake Bygdin. As a mainly touring district, there are no suitable bases.

MAPS

CAP 325M sh.2 Central Norway I covers the area and approaches. SK produce a special tourist map at 100M with useful superimposed information including marked trails, distance times and huts. Despite being the most popular mountain area in Norway, the Jotunheimen was one of the last areas to have the modern 50M series, only completed in 1986.

1517 I	Tyin		1617 IV	Gjende
1517 IV	Hurrungane		1618 I	Vågå
1518 II	Galdhøpiggen		1618 II	Sjødalen
1518 III	Sygnefjell		1618 III	Glittertind
1617 I	Sikkilsdalen		1618 IV	Lom

GALDHØPIGGEN from SE

HUTS and other accommodation

Huts in the area are either privately owned or belong to DNT. All the self-service and unstaffed huts are opened by the standard DNT key.

Staffed huts:	beds	Map No.	4-fig. ref.
Gjendebu	84	1617 IV	72-13
Gjendesheim	129	1617 IV	90-18
Glitterheim	120	1618 III	80-32
Skogadalsbøen	82	1517 IV	47-14
Private (staffed) huts:			
Juvasshytta	75	1518 II	66-38
Leirvassbu	200	1518 II	60-24
Memurubu	100	1617 IV	80-17
Spiterstulen	140	1518 II	68-32
Torfinnsbu	40	1617 IV	78-02
Vetti	21	1517 IV	42-05
Self-service huts:			
Fannaråkhytta	32	1518 III	41-20
Olavsbu	40	1517 I	61-15
Unstaffed huts:			
Skagastølsbu	4	1517 IV	39-14
Stølsmaradalen	4	1517 IV	43-08

YH at Valdresflya, Skjolden and Sjoa.

WALKING TOURS

The area is provided with a network of well marked summer trails; it is easy to work out many possible routes. For the backpacker not restricted to huts there is even greater scope, as well as cost savings. Popular tours include:

1. **Gjendesheim to Vetti** (about 10 days)
Gjendesheim - Memurubu (via the Besseggen ridge) - Glitterheim - Spiterstulen (via Glittertind) - ascent/descent of Galdhøpiggen - Leirvassbu - Krossbu (includes gl. crossing + rope, guide available in season) - Fannaråkhytta - Skogadalsbøen - Vetti.

2. **Fagernes to Gjendesheim** (about 5 days)
Fagernes - Svarthammar - Storkvelbvu - Oskampen - Sikkilsdalsseter - Gjendesheim.

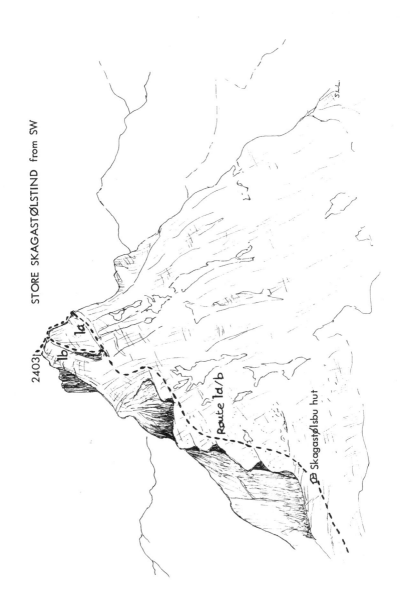

STORE SKAGASTØLSTIND from SW

2403

1b

1a

Route 1d/b

Skagastølsbu hut

S.L.L.

MOUNTAIN ASCENTS

Little has been published about climbing in the Jotunheimen and infomation previously available is not always reliable - in particular the route gradings. The Hurrungane has a detailed climbing guide by NTK (in Norwegian and part English), but for other districts a pioneering spirit is useful. Some suggested ascents arranged by districts follow.

Western

STORE SKAGASTØLSTIND 2403m.

Known as "Storen". A superb mountain, perhaps the finest in Norway, with more than 14 recorded routes. The climbs are mostly long and go from II to VI+. The rock is mainly excellent gabbro.

1a. Normal route by SW ridge, Hjørnet and Heftyes Renne. III/IV. From Skagastølsdalen go SE to the col and Skagastølsbu hut, known as "Hytta på Bandet" - very full in summer. Ascend the ill-defined and partly cairned broad ridge for 600m., hard scrambling (I/II); it is advisable to keep well L after the first section to avoid difficult steep slabs. The upper part of the mountain forms a large tower with a prominent gully splitting the SW face - this is Andrews Renne. Below this gully a large ledge slants up R (SE); ascend this to an exposed corner high above Slingsby gl. This corner is the Hjørnet and should not be confused with another similar corner some 140m. lower. An awkward traverse, followed by steep slab to foot of impending wall (II/III). A steep polished chimney, Heftyes Renne, is awkward to start, but eases after 15m. (III/IV). Scramble to S summit, then cross gap to the main summit. Minimum time, 4h. from hut. Variations to L and R of the Heftyes Renne are III+ and IV+. Descend from S summit initially with easy climbing, then abseil to large ledge. Now reverse normal route.

1b. By Andrews Renne, III/III+. The prominent gully mentioned in 1a. From the slanting ledge leading up to the Hjørnet, traverse L, then R and finally up to gap between S and main summit. Fairly good rock, but loose on ledges. 4-5 h. from hut. Descent as for 1a.

NORDRE SKAGASTØLSTIND 2167m.

2. N flank, grade I, scrambling. From Turtagrø follow main path into Skagastølsdalen and to the small tarn near NTK hut. Go L, aiming for gap between Kolnosi and N Skagastølstind. From gap scramble and walk up steep flank to summit, 3h.

STORE DYRHAUGSTIND 2147m.

3. NE ridge, hard scrambling, I/II. A fine central viewpoint for the Hurrungane group. Start from Skagastølsdalen or Ringsdalen. By

STORE AUSTABOTTIND from N

steep walking onto ridge, broad at first but narrowing into fine scramble, 3-4h. Can be continued to Midtre Dyrhaugstind (2134m.) and Søre Dyrhaugstind (2072m.), 30 min. From here it is possible to descend the W flank to Ringsbreen gl. for Ringsdalen, or reverse the route.

STORE RINGSTIND   2124m.

4. E flank, a gl. crossing and steep snow. From Ringsdalen follow a path to the moraine. Go up to the L, some paint markings, unstable boulders. Traverse R to Ringsbreen above the level of the ice-fall. Go R (W) up the gl, once easy but now shrunk and heavily crevassed, at times gaining easier rock ridge on L, 4-5h.

STORE SOLEITIND   2083m.

5. W flank, a walk. Take road from Turtagrø towards Øvre Årdal, until shortly before it descends to the toll gate. Head SE over the fjell and round tarns until the flank becomes steep and stony. Get on to and follow broad ridge to summit, 3-4h.

STORE AUSTABOTTIND   2204m.

6. W ridge, II. Take road as in 5 above, until it descends into the Berdalen. Follow ridge easily up to Vestre Austabottind (2100m.), 3h. Descend into gap, then 2 pitches of II to continue; easy angled ridge at first then long gully to R of ridge, followed by steep snow on to a saddle (ice-axe), II. Follow airy ridge to main summit, II. Conditions very variable, 2-3h$\frac{1}{2}$ Descend same way.

The Hurrungane group also has 3 excellent long ridge traverses with climbing up to IV. These are all serious expeditions. The ridges are: Skagastølsryggen, Styggedalsryggen and Maradalsryggen.

STORE SMØRSTABBTIND   2208m.

7a. N ridge, ungraded, probably easy. From Krossbu go round the flank of Leirbreen gl. in a NE direction, keeping S of the Leirvatnet (1682m.). Follow N ridge directly to top. Descend same way. Round trip, 5h.

7b. SE ridge, probably IV. From Leirvassbu go down Leirdalen and SW onto Storbreen gl. Keeping L, head for the foot of SE ridge. Two pitches of III/IV followed by an easier section then a steep wall, before easy continuation to summit. Time not known. Descend by stony S face using gully to get onto the Leirbreen gl.

STETIND   2020m.

8. S ridge, ungraded, easy scramble. Remarkable panorama. From Leirvassbu follow path W into Gravdalen for about 1$\frac{1}{2}$km. Go N up the steep flank, which narrows into ridge. From S summit (1987m.) follow narrow ridge to main summit. Ascent and descent, about 5h.

HURRUNGANE peaks from NE

STORE KNUTHOLSTIND 2341m.

1a. S ridge, II/III. From Gjendebu go S and ascend steeply into Svartdalen as far as the lake beneath the mountain, 2h. This point can also be reached from Torfinnsbu in about 3h. From here a fairly obvious diagonal rake leads to a skyline gap at the foot of the S ridge, 1h. Ascend broad flank at first, soon narrowing to a fine crest giving 275m. of scrambling and easy climbing, exposed on E side, 1h. Descend by W face over broken rocky walls, ledges and boulders.

1b. Traverse to Nordligste Knutholstind (2140m.), III/III+. From summit continue along ridge in N direction, descending some awkward sections, mainly II, with considerable exposure on R into the Knuthols cirque. After $1\frac{1}{2}$–2h. and a tower of III, the ridge broadens and swings R (NE) towards a rounded summit, pt.2185. Ignore this and traverse the stony flank to the prominent tower of the final N top, best done by W face and a final corner on good rock (III/III+). Abseil back down same corner, then descend into Svartdalen, keeping slightly N to avoid steep slabs.

KALVEHØGDI 2178m.

2. E ridge, ungraded, probably easy. From Torfinnsbu take lakeside path E towards Valdresflya YH and to Vestre Repefonnbekken; this is followed up the steep flank, possibly snowy, to the gap W of Rasletind. Turn W and follow the winding ridge for about 2km. to summit, 4–5h. Continue to higher Vestre Kalvåhøgda (2208m.), 1h. Descend the same way or go E over Rasletind (2105m.) and down to Valdresflya.

TJØRNHOLSTIND 2330m.

3a. N ridge, ungraded, estimated an easy scramble. From Memurubu it is possible to get a boat across Gjende lake to the foot of the steep N flanks of the mountain. Ascend until the ground narrows into ridge; impressive views into N Tjørnholet cirque on L. Ridge swings E just before summit, 5h. Descend the same way or by 3b.

3b. SE face, a walk; has been done on ski. From route 51 a little S of Gjendesheim cross Leirungsåi river (bridge), head W over the Steinflyi fjell, cross the safe and easy Steinflybreen gl, finally ascending steep S flank to summit, 6h.

SLETTMARKPIGGEN 2163m.

4. N & W ridges, good scramble, I/II. From Gjendebu take the path SW towards Eidsbugarden until shortly after it crosses the Vesleåi river (about 4km.). Head S steeply at first, then easily to the foot of the

steep face and ridge leading to the N summit. Ascend partly in a steep snow gully, partly the broken rocks on its L. Above this, long slopes of easy snow and rock lead to N summit at c.2000m. On the L side an enormous overhung wall drops to Slettmarkbreen gl. - no route known. Turning E, scramble awkwardly down and across a wall to the col before the main summit (I/II). Pleasant scramble for some 100m. to the summit, exposed on L, with final interesting move onto very airy summit block, 5h. Descend the same way; do not stray too far R descending N ridge.

RAUDDALSEGGA (Store Austre Rauddalstind) 2168m.

5. E ridge, grade not known. From Olavsbu take the Gjendebu path along upper Rauddalen to foot of E ridge. Ascend this to long, narrow and exposed summit ridge. Estimated, 3-4h. Descend the same way.

STØLSNOSTIND 2074m.

6. E ridge, grade not known. A striking pyramid. From Vetti go E up Morka-Koldedalen, on to the Stølnosi gl. and so to the foot of the narrow E ridge. Ascend this by scrambling, possibly climbing, to top, 4h.

URANOSTIND 2157m.

7. N face, probably scrambling. From Skogadalsbøen go S then E up Uradalen to its head and the pass at 1438m. Go up NE by the steep flank to col below N face. Ascend to summit, 8h. Possible to traverse easily S along ridge to Søre Uranostind (2048m.). Reverse route for descent, or go down S ridge from Søre U. - this has been done but no details are available. This mountain can also be ascended from Eidsbugarden or Tyinholmen.

North and Central

SURTNINGSSUI 2368m.

1. W flank, cairned path. From Memurubu follow Memurudalen W, then N for almost 8km. before the path turns E and works steeply up to the summit, 5h. An alternative is to take the Glittertind path for 2km, then break off NW across awkward terrain to ascend the steep S ridge with some scrambling.

NAUTGARDSTIND 2258m.

2. E ridge, a walk; can also be skied. From Glitterheim go E across bridge over river Veo. Do not follow main path to Gjendesheim; instead go NE then S to a pass at 1731m. above Tjørnholtjarn. Now take broad flank to E, narrowing to a first top called Nautgardsoksla, 2089m. Continue SE to main summit with fine views into cirque, 3 h.

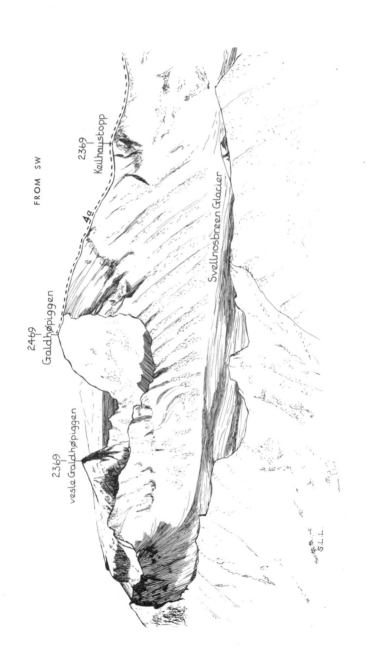

FROM SW

2369
Kalhaustopp

4a

2469
Galdhøpiggen

2369
vesle Galdhøpiggen

Svellnosbreen Glacier

S.L.L.

GLITTERTIND 2464m.

3. Traverse E-W, walking and some steep snow. From Glitterheim go W to Nedre Steinbuvatnet, then ascend steep slopes NW, gaining some 700m. height. Swing W onto snowy ridge leading to main top at 2452m. and summit ice-cap just above, heavily corniced at times to N, 3h. Descend the same way or continue W along ridge and down to Spiterstulen. Difficult navigation on upper section in mist. After the snowy upper section, follow cairns and path. Where they steepen to wind down a rocky ridge, it is better to descend an easy wide gully to the N side. Continue easily, well marked to the Skauta river ford. Finally steeply down into Visdalen, $3\frac{1}{2}$h.

GALDHØPIGGEN 2469m.

Usually considered the highest mountain in Norway and consequently something of a pilgrimage by all comers.

4a. E flank, a walk with some steep snow. From Spiterstulen cross the bridge over the Visa and ascend the steep E slopes, firstly winding up the track towards Juvasshytta, then heading W up the prominent Svellnosa (2053m.). The broad ridge is followed up and down, past the Keilhaus Topp (2369m.), and after a final dip the main summit, 4-5h. Outstanding panorama on a clear day. Descend the same way.

4b. NE face, a walk with gl. crossing - rope and axe/crampons needed. From Juvasshytta head SW to the Styggebreen glacier; many guided parties. Go up steep snowy ridge R on to main summit, $2\frac{1}{2}$-3h. Descend the same way or by 4a.

There are several other ways of varying grades up the mountain including mixed rock and ice climbs.

STYGGEHØ 2213m.

5. NE ridge, scrambling, I/II. From Spiterstulen cross the bridge over the Visa, turn immediately S along the bank, wading the outlets from Svellnosbreen and Tverråbreen gls. with difficulty (best early in day). Wind up W through boulders and scrub to the ridge, broad at first then narrowing into a pleasant scramble with a steep finish, 4h.

MEMURUTINDEN 2364m.

A group of impressive summits linked into a long complex ridge, forming: Sydligste (2140m.), Vestre (2243 and 2280m.), Store (2364m.), and Austre (2301m.).

6a. Store Memurutind by N ridge from Veokar. Easy, can also be skied. From Spiterstulen take main path S towards Leirvassbu, as far as the Hellstuguåi torrent. Do not cross the bridge; go up E to the Hellstugubreen gl, usually bare and easy in its lower part - crevasses later. Keep L on gl. until you can ascend very steeply to a gap in the high ridge (this is Veoskar). Follow ridge S to main summit, 5h. It is possible to continue along to other tops of the group, or descend.

6b. Leirhø (2330m.). S ridge, from Veoskar, easy. From Spiter-stulen ascend as for 6a to the Veoskar. Turn N and go up easily to the main summit, 4-4½h. From 6a or 6b, descend the same way.

URDADALSTINDEN 2116m.

7. A 3km. ridge, the N - S traverse is II/III. From Spiterstulen, take the Leirvassbu path S to the junction with Urdadalen, about 2½h. Cross the Urdadala river with difficulty (easier higher) and work up rocks onto N ridge. This becomes narrow and exposed, also loose (II), up to main summit, 2½h. Descend same way or continue along the un-dulating ridge over tops 2060 and 2017, scrambling and climbing with pitches of II/III. From final top descend E into Urdadalen; plus 2-3h.

KYRKJA 2032m.

8. S ridge, short pleasant scramble. From Leirvassbu take the Ola-vsbu path S, keeping to the edge of Leirvatn lake and so to top of the pass (Hogvaglen). Break off E up stony slopes, bypassing or going over Kyrkjeoksla. The S ridge is directly ahead; the rock is sound and cle-aner than normal, 2½h.

The E and SE Jotunheimen district, although an attractive upland area and excellent for walking or skiing in a quieter and wilder environment, offers no summits normally ascended for their own merit.

red fox

Rondane & Dovre

WHILE really adjoining areas, for our purposes the 2 have sufficient in common to be considered as a single unit; a typical Central Mountains area presenting a large zone of almost unbroken upland, parts of which are quite remote. It is well known for walking and ski-touring, also for pleasant and relatively easy mountain ascents. There are 15 summits over the magical 2000m. mark. Probably the most famous is Snøhetta (2286m.) in Dovre - the highest Scandinavian summit outside the Jotunheimen. Some climbing has been done in both Rondane and Dovre, with further potential in the latter, although some tracts are difficult of access.

Many parts of the overall area are quite outstanding for wildlife. Both flora and fauna are now protected by reserves and 2 National Parks, known as Rondane and Dovre, 572 sq. km. and about 400 sq. km. respectively. Wild reindeer abound in both districts and Dovre seems likely to have the highest density of wolverines in Norway. Musk ox were introduced into Dovre from Greenland earlier this century; they have thrived, even spreading into Sweden. The Fokstumyra wetlands are internationally famous for their birdlife, particularly waders.

Climatically this area is typical of E Norway, being greatly protected by mountain groups to the W - particularly the Rondane district which has a rain-shadow climate and no glaciers. NW Dovre is less protected and is wetter with heavier snowfall and a few remnant gls, but most of this district too is relatively dry. In winter the combination of wind and infrequent snow can occasionally result in extensive areas of ridged icy snow.

The boundaries are: in the N the valley of Sunndalen and route 16 from Sunndalsøra to Oppdal; in the E the E6 from Oppdal to Hjerkinn borders Dovre and route 29 from Hjerkinn to Folldal; continuing along route 27 to the beautiful Lake Atnasjøen borders Rondane; the long western border in reality runs from NW to the southern apex and follows the E6, NW from Ringebu to Dombås, then the E69 to upper Romsdalen where a line roughly N can be taken through Lake Eikesdal.

APPROACHES

From Oslo there is an excellent rail link, with the line running up the W side of Rondane, then E after Dombås, forming the border of the two districts, Rondane and Dovre. Otta (for Rondane) takes $3\frac{1}{2}$ h. and $4\frac{1}{2}$ h.

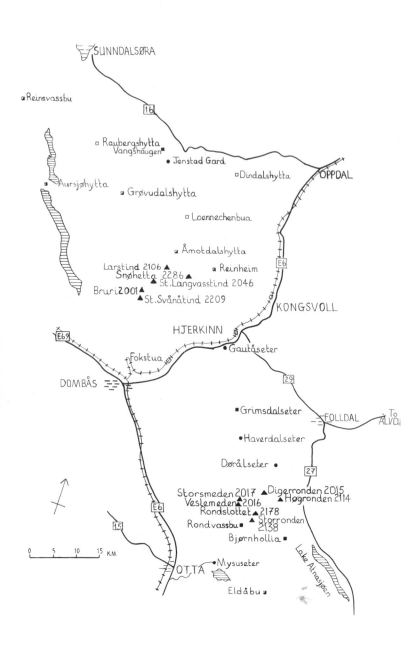

to Hjerkinn (for Dovre). Another line from Oslo to Røros is useful for E Rondane, taking $4\frac{1}{2}$h. to Atna or 5h. to Alvdal – onward link by bus or taxi.

From Oslo it is also possible to take buses to various starting points on the edges of the area.

Using your own transport from Oslo take the E6 N, which follows the Gudbrandsdalen for most of the way to Ringebu (253km.). For E Rondane break off here and follow route 220 to Lake Atnasjøen (46km.), then route 27 to various starting points. From Ringebu continue N on the E6 to Otta (55km.) and Dombås (102km.), where the E69 can be taken NW for access to W parts of Dovre. From Dombås again along E6 for other parts of Dovre; Hjerkinn and Kongsvoll are starting points.

BASES

As usual in S Norway the tourer is well provided with more than 20 huts and numerous readily accessible starting points for excursions. For walking and climbing there are 2 useful hut bases from which most of the highest summits can be attained, but neither can be reached by car. In Dovre, Åmotsdalshytta is reached from Kongsvoll or Hjerkinn, via the hut at Reinheim, 2 days with heavy loads. In Rondane, Rondvassbu is reached after a 10km. walk from the roadhead at Mysuseter.

MAPS

CAP 325M sh.2 Central Norway I covers the area and approaches. SK issues 2 special maps at 100M – Rondane and Snøhetta. The 50M maps are relatively new.

1419 I	Storskrymten	1519 IV	Snøhetta
1419 II	Dombås	1520 III	Oppdal
1419 III	Lesjaskog	1619 III	Alvdal
1420 II	Romfo	1718 I	Rondane
1420 III	Sunndalsøra	1718 IV	Otta
1519 I	Einunna	1818 I	Sollia
1519 II	Folldal	1818 IV	Atnasjøen
1519 III	Hjerkinn		

HUTS and other accommodation

DNT operate all huts in Rondane, except for private staffed huts. In Dovre, huts are controlled by DNT, KNT (Kristiansund & Nordmøre Turistforening) and TT (Trondhjem Turistforening). Self-service huts are usually left unlocked or use the standard DNT key.

Rondane

Staffed huts:	beds	Map No.	4-fig. ref.
Bjørnhollia	90	1818 IV	53-61
Grimsdalshytta	34	1519 III	33-84
Rondvassbu	102	1718 I	41-61

Self-service huts:

Eldåbu	14	1818 IV	51-47

Private staffed huts:

Breisjøseter	no info-	1818 IV	65-70
Dørålseter	mation	1718 I	42-74
Flatseter	available	1519 II	62-77
Follandsvangen		1619 III	67-80
Gautaseter	28	1519 III	28-96
Haverdalseter	20	1818 I	34-78
Nyhusseter	8	1619 III	66-80

Dovre

Staffed hut: Vangshaugen	40	1420 II	97-34
Pvte staffed hut: Jenstad Gard	16	1420 II	03-30

Self-service huts:

Aursjøhytta	30 KNT	1419 IV	76-19
Dindalshytta	12 TT	1520 III	17-34
Grøvudalshytta	20 KNT	1419 I	94-23
Reinheim	26 DNT	1519 IV	18-12
Reinsvassbu	8 DNT	1420 III	67-35
Åmotdalshytta	21 KNT	1419 I	10-14

Unstaffed huts:

Loennechenbua	4 KNT	1419 I	09-22
Raubergshytta	8 KNT	1420 III	85-32

YH at Alvdal, Dalholen, Dombås, Lesjaskog, Oppdal and Sunndal-søra.

WALKING TOURS

1. Alvdal to Hjerkinn (about 7 days)
Alvdal - Breisjøseter - Bjørnhollia - Rondvassbu - Dørålseter - Grimsdalshytta - Hjerkinn. From Hjerkinn it is only a 2 h. link to Kongsvoll and into Dovre.

From Bjørnhollia a good alternative is to link up with the Rondane to Lillehammer trail, finally using the huts of Lillehammer & Omland Turistforening (LOT), as follows:

Bjørnhollia – Eldåbu – Gråhøgdbu – Breitjønnbu – Gopollen (LOT) –
Djupsliseter (LOT) – Nordseter/Lillehammer.

2. Kongsvoll to Vike (about 6 days)
Kongsvoll – Reinheim – Åmotsdalshytta – Grøvudalshytta – Aursjøhytta
– Reinsvassbu – Vike. This continues into the Romsdal area (Grøvdal)
via Hoemsbu.

ASCENTS

Rondane

RONDSLOTTET 2178m.
1. A walk to the highest summit in Rondane, 7h. round trip. From
Rondvassbu take the Bjørnhollia path (E) for a short way. Break off NE
to foot of broad W ridge of Storronden. Leave this path for another N
and NE into Rondholet cirque. Steep ascent up scree and boulders to S
top (2044m.). Follow ridge N for about one km. to main summit. Impressive wall on R into Storbotn cirque. Descend the same way.

STORRONDEN 2138m.
2. W ridge; walking, about 5h. round trip. From Rondvassbu start
as for 1 above, but carry on E up the broad stony ridge with a steeper
section before summit. Return same way or continue fairly easily to
Rondslottet S top along ridge running NW.

VESLEMEDEN 2016m.
3. E flank and ridge. Cairned path. From Rondvassbu go W across
lake (boat) and take path N towards Dørålseter, ascending Rondhalsen.
The path divides: take NW direction up the steep flank, culminating
in narrow ridge to summit, about 4h. Descend same way or traverse
NE ridge to Storsmeden.

STORSMEDEN 2017m.
4. NE ridge from Veslemeden; easy climbing/scrambling. As for 3
above, then take steep ridge SW down to col at c.1800m. and ascend
to summit, rather loose in places, about 1½h. This outing can be continued along N ridge for 1½km. to N summit (1922m.). Then descend
to join the Langhølet – Dørålen path. Long day.

HØGRONDEN 2114m.
5. NE ridge, cairned path, 7-8h. round trip. From Dørålseter walk
up main valley (SW) and cross to true R bank of river Dørái after about
one km. Then go SE and E along path, some cairns, rising gradually for
several km. up to the impressive Midbotn cirque. Pass the lake and go
up the NE ridge very steeply to summit. Descend same way or reverse 6.

6. Digerronden to Høgronden ridge traverse. Moderate scrambling.

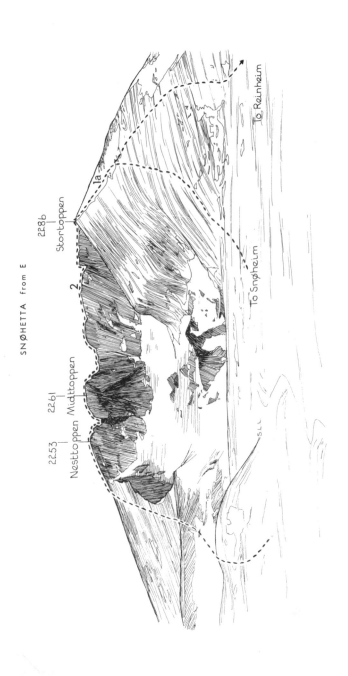

SNØHETTA from E

2286
Stortoppen

1a

To Reinheim

To Snøheim

2
2261
Midttoppen
2253
Nesttoppen

From Dorålseter as for no.5, but continue on L bank for about one km. further, until path to Rondvassbu leads S. Take this until opposite W ridge of Digerronden, then find crossing point on river and ascend the large blocks steeply to summit (2015m.). Now the good scrambly ridge, loose in parts, over Midtronden (2060m.) and finally to Høgronden in about 6h. Reverse ridge or descend no.5.

The rock of Rondane is of a sandstone type known as sparagmite which weathers into large rectangular blocks. It is not stable and although some of the headwalls of the cirque look impressively suitable for rock climbing, the rock quality is suspect.

Dovre

The rock of Dovre is a very complex mixture; oversimplified, mainly it is gneiss and the sandstone sparagmite. The general effect is sounder rock than in Rondane.

SNØHETTA 2286m.

1a. E ridge, marked path. From Reinheim go S fairly steeply up the valley side until it levels out. Take E ridge markers to summit, about 3h. An unsightly structure mars the main summit but an adjoining top affords a fine panorama. Descend the same way or by 1b, below.

1b. N ridge; walking and scrambling, ice axe useful. From Åmotsdalshytta take the Reinheim path for about one km, then strike up SE, keeping E of the big cirque between Snøhetta and Larstind. Climb the ridge steeply to snowfield and traverse this partly to summit ridge, 3-4h. Descend the same way, or by 1a. Or traverse, as below.

2. Snøhetta Traverse. A classic outing, considered best E-W, also done often in winter. II/III. From Reinheim or Åmotsdalshytta attain summit (Stortoppen) by 1a or 1b, 3-4h. Descend to gap and proceed over pinnacles. Difficulties are mainly on W pinnacle known as Hettpiggen, from the gap Vest Skar (II/III); from Stortoppen to Vesttoppen, 2-3h. Descend SE ridge to Reinheim or go down S flank to path leading N to Åmotsdalshytta.

To make a longer traverse continue from Vesttoppen along the ridge Larseggen E and N, and over Larstind back to Åmotsdalshytta. Much of this is good scrambling, but there are climbing sections, probably up to grade IV. Allow at least 3h.

Snøhetta also has technical possibilities on the E walls of the pinnacles (up to 300m.).

LARSTIND 2106m.

3. N ridge, hard scramble, I/II. From Åmotsdalshytta go SE and work up onto pt.1945, steep and broken. Follow ridge easily at first,

steeper and more exposed on nearing the top; 2-3h.

STORE LANGVASSTIND 2046m.

4a. W ridge, probably moderate climbing. From Åmotsdalshytta go along the lake SW to where a path cuts up S to Langvatnet. Now follow path along lake until beneath W ridge; ascend this steeply to top.

4b. SE ridge, probably difficult climbing. From Åmotsdalshytta by 4a only as far as the start for Langvatnet, then up a path steeply E to a tarn at 1640m. Go round this and climb steep SW ridge.

SVÅNÅTINDEN 2209m.

5. Long and complex ridge group comprising Store Svånåtind at the apex, Bruri (2001m.), and 2 other tops at 2078m. and 2004m.

From Åmotsdalshytta follow 4a above, and continue along Langvatnet to its end. Walk up and round in a SE direction into a large shelving snowy bowl, fairly steep, but becoming easier near the ridge. Go to main or other tops as desired (except Bruri which is harder), 4-5h. This route can be done on ski.

elk

C. FJORD RANGES

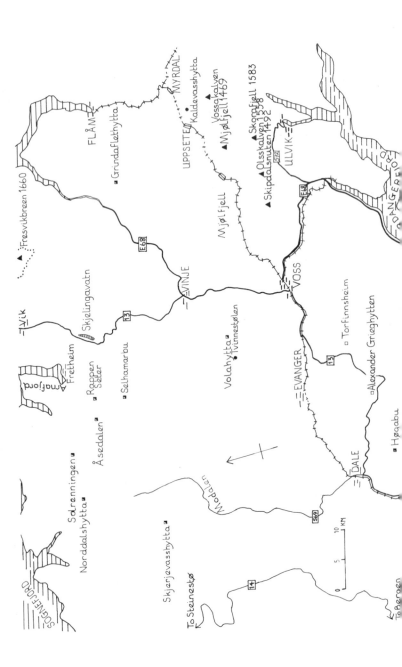

SOGNEFJORD

Norddalshytta ∎
Sørenningen ∎

Skjærjavasshytta ∎

To Steinestø ←

To Bergen ←

Åsedalen ∎

Rappen Sæter ∎
Fretheim

⊐Vik

Arnafjord

Selhamarbu ∎

Skjelingavatn

⊟13

Fresvikbreen 1660 ▲

GrundaFlæthytta ∎

FLÅM

MYRDAL
UPPSETE ∎ ● Kaldevasshytta
Vossakalven ▲
▲Mjølfjell 1469

Skorafjell 1583 ▲
▲Olsskalven 1558
Skipdalsnuten 1492 ▲

ULVIK ⊟572

HARDANGERFJORD

Mjølfjell

⊟E68

VINJE

Modalen

⊟E68

Volahytta ∎
● Tvinnastølen

EVANGER

VOSS

⊟13

□ Torfinnsheim

□Alexander Grieghytten

Høgabu ∎

DALE

⊟E68

⊟↑

0   5   10 KM

Stølsheimen & Voss/Mjølfjell

THESE 3 districts are closely connected topographically and to a great extent make up a natural unit, although their eastern boundaries do merge into the Central Mountains region. It is a very varied and attractive area, deeply dissected by valleys and strikingly indented by deep fjords. Although the maximum height of the mountains is not great, no summit exceeding 1800m., close proximity to the sea and low lying valleys gives an impression of much greater height. Several remnant ice-caps exist; one is fairly large - Fresvikbreen, rising to 1660m. and some 25 sq.km. in area.

The immensely long Sognefjord provides the natural boundary in the N, with its long arm Aurlandsfjorden stretching S and providing the start of the eastern boundary. This continues S along the Flåm-Myrdal railway, then roughly to the head of Hardangerfjord. This long fjord in the S is another natural border; in the W there is no obvious boundary other than the fall to lower ground.

This is another good area for walking tours and it is practical to link routes in all 3 districts to form a long trek. Deep valleys make the area less suitable for ski-touring, except in the E. The Mjølfjell district is quite well known to a number of British walkers, but few have visited Stølsheimen. The latter is mainly used by visitors from Bergen who patronise the good network of self-service huts.

Valleys and lower levels are noted for their lush vegetation, with moss and lichen growth especially impressive, reflecting climatic conditions. It is an area of very high precipitation and Bergen is one of the wettest places in Norway. Snowfall is also heavy; some parts of the area measure the annual fall in metres. However, the climate is exceptionally varied with long hot spells in some summers. While the climate might be termed mild, in most years the deep valleys have recorded extremely low temperatures - in Voss down to -50C.

APPROACHES

As the whole area is fairly close to Bergen there are good public transport services. By rail in just over 1 h. to Voss and 2 h. to Mjølfjell. A useful and spectacular branch line runs from Myrdal to Flåm.

By sea, coastal ferries into Sognefjord are rapid and regular. Noreide takes $4\frac{1}{2}$ h. from Bergen, then a local link to Stølsheimen. From

Bergen there are bus services N into Stølsheimen, also E to the Voss/Mjølfjell districts and further N to E Stølsheimen.

With a car take the E68 to Voss (167km.), passing a number of starting points for the Voss fjells. Alternatively take the E68 to Trengereid (41km.), then route 13 to Voss (84km.), passing the northern starting points to Voss fjells and southern ones for Stølsheimen.

From a point just before Voss on the E68, take a narrow road leading E to Mjølfjell (33km.). After the YH a very narrow, bumpy dirt road continues for about 10km. as far as Uppsete.

From Voss continue N on the E68, then route 13 as far as Vik, passing starting points for E Stølsheimen. Stay on E68 for the furthest E mountains. From Vik minor roads W go into Arnafjorden and to Fretheim for N Stølsheimen.

For W Stølsheimen leave Bergen on route 14 to Steinestø - Knarvik ferry, and stay on route 14 until tiny roads lead E.

BASES

Stølsheimen, being a touring district, does not have any suitable bases for overall exploration. The Voss/Mjølfjell districts have 2 possible centres. In the W the highly developed resort of Voss has complete facilities and is useful if you are prepared to drive some distance to the mountains. In the E the village of Mjølfjell is well placed and has a variety of accommodation and a useful shop (with petrol).

MAPS

CAP 325M sh.2 Central Norway I depicts the entire area. There are special tourist maps for Voss at 50M and 25M, also a 25M sheet for Mjølfjell. At present the 50M survey maps for the area include some old sheets, indicated (O). New maps should be issued by 1988.

1215 I	Strandebarm (O)	1316 III	Voss
1216 I	Eksingedal (O)	1316 IV	Myrkdalen
1216 II	Evanger (O)	1317 II	Leikanger
1217 II	Høyanger (O)	1317 III	Kvamsøy
1316 I	Gudvangen	1416 III	Myrdal
1316 II	Ulvik	1416 IV	Aurland

HUTS and other accommodation

Huts are controlled by 3 organisations: DNT, Bergen Turlag and Voss Utferdslag. Huts are either shut with DNT standard key or left unlocked.

Stølsheimen

| Self-service huts: | beds | Map No. | 4-fig. ref. |
| Norddalshytta | 26 | 1217 II | 36–67 |

84

Rappan Seter	16	1316 IV	53–61
Skjerjevasshytta	20	1216 I	29–56
Solrenningen	16	1217 II	45–67
Selhamarbu	26	1316 IV	51–56
Volahytta	12	1316 III	53–36
Åsedalen	20	1316 IV	49–62

YH at Vangsnes.

Voss/Mjølfjell

Self-service: Grindaflethytta	12	1316 I	86–47
Høgabu	32	1216 II	31–14
Unstaffed: Alexander Grieghytta	32	1216 II	39–14
Jønshøgdi	42	1215 I	34–97
Kaldevasshytta	4	1416 III	95–31
Torfinnsheim	34	1316 III	48–17
Tvinnestølen	7	1316 III	56–36

YH at Mjølfjell and Voss.

WALKING TOURS

1. Skjelingavatn to Modalen (about 6 days).
A tour covering much of Stølsheimen E to W. Skjelingavatn (route 13, about 30 km. N of Vinje) – Rappan Seter – Åsedalen – Solrenningen – Norddalshytta – Skjerjevasshytta – Modalen.

2. Mjølfjell district round tour (about 5 days)
Mjølfjell – Ulvik Hallingskeid – Uppsete – Grindaflethytta – Mjølfjell.

ASCENTS

Stølsheimen district

FRESVIKBREEN 1660m.
Glacier ascent, rope, axe, crampons advisable. Easiest approach from Øvstedalen in the S, alternatively from Fresvik in the E.

Mjølfjell district

VOSSASKAVLEN glacier
Walk, 8–9 h. round trip. From Mjølfjell take the rough track to Uppsete, then the paint marked path rising E. At a junction take the Hallingskeid direction and follow to Kaldevatn lake. Do not take the path to Kaldevasshytta; instead follow a faintly marked path N then E round the lake, ascending steeply via ledges. Finally traverse to foot of gl. and ascend keeping L, fairly steep but safe.

85

SKORAFJELL   1583m.

8h. round trip walk. From Mjølfjell take the Uppsete track as far as the junction to Slondal; take latter track, cross the bridge and go up to Lake Slondalsvatnet. At S end of the lake follow small path leading SW to beyond the pass, when it becomes practical to ascend broad ridge leading S to summit. After descending the same ridge go W and NW back to Mjølfjell, recrossing main river about 1½km. W of Mjølfjell station.

MJØLFJELL   1469m.

5h. round trip walk. From Mjølfjell cross the bridge between station and YH and follow path S into Mjølbotn cirque; ascend steep slopes SE to main summit. Descend the same way.

There are a number of other interesting walking ascents in the area – to Olsskavlen (1558m.), Seldalsnuten (1547m.) and Skipadalsnuten (1492m.) among others.

The Voss fjells contain a number of relatively minor summits, most of which have easy ascents. Routes can easily be plotted with the aid of a map. The huts at Torfinnsheim and Alexander Grieg provide good bases for exploration of this group.

Numerous long slabs and high walls flank the many fjords of the area with tremendous possibilities for rock climbing. A certain amount has been done, mainly by climbers from Bergen, but also noted are a few British ascents. The rock is heavily worn and polished by ice and routes of a high grade can be expected.

musk ox

Jostedal - Breheimen - Ålfot

GLACIERS and ice-caps are the dominant features of this area. One major ice-cap, a further 10 large ice-caps and a number of smaller ones, altogether cover about 800 sq. km. The ice attains its apex on Harbardsbreen (2010m.) and its lowest point on Jostedalsbreen at 295m. The highest summit of the area is Lodalskåpa (2083m.), still virtually a nunatak, despite the recession of ice.

This is a unique area within mainland Europe. It offers walking and ski tours of a very unusual nature, as almost all involve the crossing of at least one ice-cap. Breheimen means "home of the glaciers". On most of the gl., ice axe, crampons and rope are advisable; even in winter roped skiing is recommended in some places. Because of the additional mountaineering skills required the area is not popular with the average Norwegian tourer and can be expected to be quiet and peaceful. This is reflected in the hut network which is sparse, with most huts small.

The Jostedalsbreen with a surface area of 486 sq. km. is easily the largest ice-cap gl. in Norway and on the continent of Europe. It projects no less than 24 valley gl. tongues, of which the Tunbergdals flow is the longest in Norway. The lower parts of these tongues are still receding, but the status of the upper ice-cap is uncertain. The western flanks in particular are extremely steep and wildly beautiful; Lodalen is probably the finest of all. The waterfalls and rivers are amongst the most powerful in Norway and because of this the area is now under threat by the insatiable demand for hydro-electric power.

Climatically the district is little different to the rest of the Fjord region, being subject to a heavy annual precipitation, although a higher proportion here falls as snow. Because of the altitude of the ice-caps and the volume of snow it is practical to ski-tour here later than in any other southern and central parts of Norway; into June on the Jostedalsbreen. As well as having a lot of bad weather, the area is subject to frequent weather changes.

The N boundary is marked by the long and attractive Nordfjord, then route 15 over into Ottadalen; in the S it is the Sognefjord and its northern arms; in the E the area merges into the Jotunheimen, but Leirdalen and route 55 will serve as limits; in the W it is merely lower ground, with the Ålfot gl. and satellites situated further W.

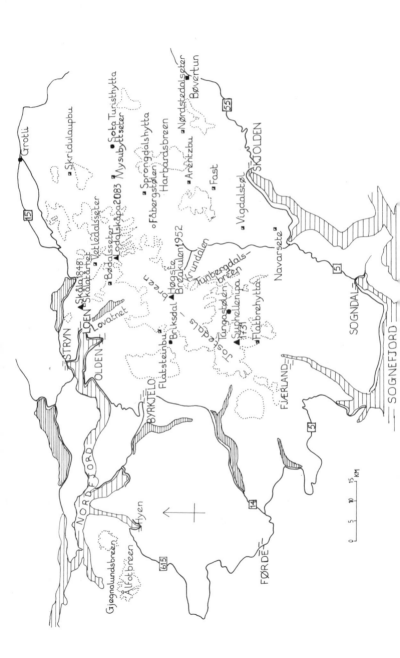

APPROACHES

From Bergen by ship, all year services into Sognefjord and Nordfjord; 6h. into Sogne and about 19h. into upper Nordfjord.

By rail from Bergen to Myrdal (2h.), branch line to Flåm (1h.), then bus and ferry links into S of area.

By rail from Oslo to Otta, then bus to Lom, finally choice of buses for N or S of the area.

By car from Bergen, follow E68, then route 13 to Voss and onwards, taking route 13 to Vangsnes (205 km.), ferry across Sogne, then E on routes 5 and 55 for S districts and Breheimen eastern districts. Or from the ferry, N on route 5 for W districts, finally along route 14.

For the Ålfot gl. and satellites the most direct way from Bergen is to take route 14 over the ferries to Førde (171 km.), then 5 and lastly 615. This approach can also be followed for the main Jostedal / Breheimen, taking route 14 after Førde to Byrkjelo (64 km.), passing some starting points, finally on route 60 to Olden/Loen/Stryn; onwards to reach the E Breheimen.

BASES

Again, the area is far too large for one or two bases to be suitable for exploring all parts. Olden, Loen or Stryn are handy for the W Jostedalsbreen if you have your own transport, as there is ready access to several valleys and higher huts. Stryn is the largest community and has most facilities. In the E the Jostedalen valley is similarly well placed but with fewer amenities and changes due to hydro-electric developments; Sogndal is the town with good services. For E Breheimen the fully staffed hut at Nørdstedalsseter provides a comfortable but fairly expensive base, although self-catering is allowed in the main season.

For Ålfot there are no huts and no local townships with significant facilities.

MAPS

CAP 325M sh.2 Central Norway I embraces the area and approaches. There is a special tourist map of Ålfot/Gloppen at the curious scale of 80M, titled Gloppen. Otherwise the whole area is covered by SK sh. in 50M.

1218 I	Nordfjordeid	1417 IV	Solvorn
1218 II	Ålfoten	1418 I	Skridulaupen
1317 I	Fjaerland	1418 II	Mørkrisdalen
1317 IV	Haukedalen	1418 III	Jostedalen
1318 I	Stryn	1418 IV	Lodalskåpa
1318 II	Brigsdalsbreen	1518 III	Sygnefjell
1318 III	Breim		

LODALSKÅPA from SW

HUTS and other accommodation

DNT operate all huts except Flatbrehytta, Flatsteinbu, Skålatårnet and Vetldalsseter (normally unlocked). All self-service and unstaffed huts are locked with the standard DNT key.

Self-service huts:	beds	Map No.	4-fig. ref.
Arentzbu	12	1418 II	23-35
Bødalsseter	12	1418 IV	99-54
Fast	7	1418 II	22-27
Flatbrehytta	16	1317 I	82-17
Navarsete	6	1417 IV	11-12
Nørdstedalsseter	27	1518 III	36-35
Skridulaupbu	4	1418 I	26-64
Skålatårnet	20	1418 IV	93-61
Sprongdalshytta	12	1418 II	20-46
Vetldalsseter	8	1418 IV	04-58
Vigdalstøl	6	1418 II	12-21
Unstaffed hut: Flatsteinbu	6	1318 II	87-42
Private staffed huts:			
Sota Turisthytte	40	1418 I	32-53
Tungastølen	16	1418 III	92-25

YH at Skjolden and Stryn.

TOURING ROUTES

1. Sota Turisthytte to Bøvertun (about 4 days)
Through E Breheimen. Sota - Sprongdalshytta - Arentzbu - Nørdstedalsseter - Bøvertun. This can be continued into the Jotunheimen area.

2. Jostedal ice-cap complete traverse NE to SW
     About 70 km., 2 to 4 days. 1st foot traverse was done in 1898 in 47 h. by Kristian Bing (Bergen) and party. 1st SW to NE foot traverse by Johannes Vigdal and Rev. H A Day in 1901.
     A superb classic ski traverse; it can also be tackled SW to NE; while it can be done on foot, this is not recommended as an alternative to skiing. The start as described below was used until 1986; now the hydro-electric works have inundated the Stygevasshytta jumping off point for the gl. Future traverses will begin further N at Grotli, probably using the hut at Skridulaupbu and the proposed new hut Mysubyttdalen, lying W of Sota. Ascents of Lodalskåpa and other nunataks can be added en route. Rope, ice axe and crampons are needed, plus considerable Nordic mountain ski-touring experience. In this exposed mountain situation good weather is important, almost essential. Good

navigation abilities required. **Approach** from Fåberg or Sota to Stygevasshytta (6h.), where the hut is now gone.

Commence skiing NW to get onto the easy tongue of Austdalsbreen, which is followed W towards Lodalskåpa. (This section will in future be approached from the N or NE). Just before Lodalskåpa ascend the difficult Småttene icefall; rope needed. Good campsite below the SW corner of Lodalskåpa (Ståleskardet). Now head S and SW across main ice-cap to its highest point, Høgste Breakulen (1952m.). Continue by Kvitekulen, Kvitekoll and Ramnane to Bings Gryte, a huge wind hole and excellent campsite. Finally go S towards the prominent nunatak of Suphellenipa, and down Flatbreen gl. tongue to Flatbrehytta; very steep and awkward descent to the fjord and Fjaerland.

There are several 1 or 2 day traverses of the Jostedalsbreen from E to W or vice versa. Because the W side gl. outlets are much steeper than the E side, routes are easiest from W to E, so that any difficulties encountered can be seen ahead in ascent. Specimen crossings are:

3.	Fåbergstølen – Bødalsseter (10–12h.)	Northern section
4.	Sprongdalshytta – Vetledalsseter (9–10h.)	Northern
5.	Tungastølen – Briksdal (12–14h.)	Central
6.	Krundalen – Kvanndalen (& Lodalen) (14h.)	Central
7.	Fjaerland – Flatbrehytta – Åmot (2 days)	Southern

At the SW end of the ice-cap the most frequented mountain excursion is an ascent of Suphellenipa (1731m.) via Flatbrehytta, Flatbreen and Suphellebreen – sometimes continued on to Bøyabreen. Taxi runs from Fjaerland hotels to beginning of footpath.

Ice axe, crampons and rope are recommended for all gl. crossings. Navigation can be difficult in conditions of low cloud. A few local guides are available although probably expensive. At the very least they should be contacted for information on ice conditions.

ASCENTS

LODALSKÅPA   2083m.

1. Normal way, walk/easy scramble in summer; safe gl., about 6h. From Bødalsseter cross the bridge and follow well marked path over 2 very steep steps; the second, Brattebakken, is some 500m. high and leads onto an easy gl. tongue (Bohrsbreen), 4h. Head SE to the rocky ridge leading to Veslekåpa (c. 1960m.). Descending slightly, ahead is the SW ridge which can be climbed with a pitch of IV then II ($1\frac{1}{2}$ h.). The ordinary route crosses snow below W face to gap beside a prominent tower; then an easy scramble SW and stony ascent to the summit. Descend the same way.

SKÅLA   1848m.

2. Strenuous walk, 6h. From Lodalen follow marked path, steep in places. As the ascent is virtually from sea-level a round trip within a day is hard. Good self-service hut on the summit, normally unlocked.

3. Skåla to Bødalsseter traverse. Gl. crossing, avalanche risk early in season, about 8h. Descend from Skåla onto Skålabreen and follow a SE direction with complex route finding until finally descending either Tindefjellbreen or Skålbreen to Bødalsseter.

All nunataks on the Jostedalsbreen have been ascended; many have good scrambling or rock climbing. There also appears to be considerable potential for rock climbing on the very steep walls of the numerous valleys radiating from the main ice-cap.

All of the subsidiary ice-caps in the Breheimen can be ascended, mostly without serious difficulties. A number of summits and nunataks give interesting rock routes. Little is known in detail.

The isolated, rarely visited Ålfot ice-cap and associated Gjengalundsbreen has little recorded information. Gjegnalund (1723m.), the highest point of the district, is best approached from Hyen. Its SW ridge gives a long rock climb of unknown grade.

great grey owl

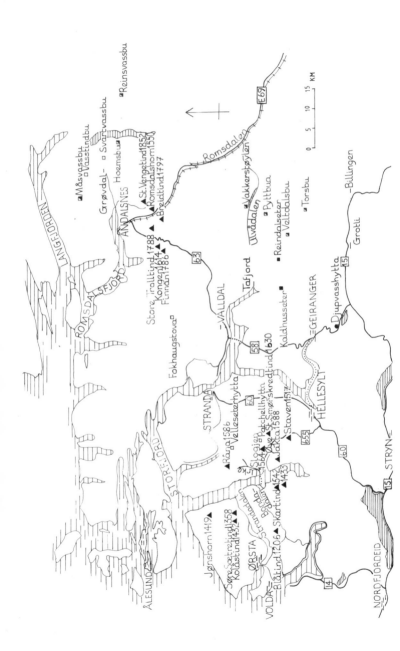

AREA 8

Sunnmøre

THIS area consists of 2 quite distinct and very different districts. In the W there is a classic fjord landscape of great beauty and variety, while in the E an inland type of mountain landscape is broken only by a few valleys. The many arms of Storfjord have split the W district into several peninsulas. The mountains here, although not exceeding 1600m. and often rising steeply from the sea, are rarely linked by ridges; instead they form a series of separate and rather impressive peaks. In the E district mountains rise to nearly 2000m., but starting points for ascents are normally about 1000m., so that they are much less spectacular in appearance.

Sunnmøre has a long tradition of rock climbing and a number of western summits are only attainable by technical routes. The W district offers excellent scope for walking, scrambling and climbing ascents, but real details are scanty. Despite its W situation there are many small gl. of the cirque type; some are quite heavily crevassed. With only a few huts, the scope for touring is non-existent. In contrast the E district is used mainly for touring, usually as part of longer trips into the neighbouring Jotunheimen, but also Dovre and Romsdal.

An unpleasant feature of the W district is the dense vegetation on the lower slopes. To reach the rock it is often necessary to fight through tangled birch scrub, with many loose and moss covered boulders extending up to the 600m. level. Perhaps surprisingly this district is not especially interesting botanically. However the open upland eastern district is very rich botanically with a fine assortment of Arctic plants.

As with all the fjord ranges this area can be very wet, especially the W district. Moreover, dense cloud cover will cause route finding problems on some of the more complicated mountains. Occasionally the summers can be very dry and long, when it would be possible to undertake many routes, as the mountains are easily accessible and seldom visited.

In the N the Storfjord and its long subsidiary fjords form a natural boundary; in the W the subsidiary Voldafjorden, then route 14 to where it meets route 15; in the S route 15; in the E the mountains merge into the western district of Romsdal (Area 9) without a distinct boundary.

APPROACHES

From Bergen by daily coastal ship (Hurtigruten) to Måløy (9 h.) or Ålesund (15 h.); onward links by bus and local ferry. Also from Bergen by boat services into Nordfjord. Express hydrofoil takes $7\frac{1}{2}$ h. to Nordfjordeid; regular boat takes $11\frac{1}{2}$ h. to Nordfjordeid and 20 h. to Stryn; onward bus links.

From Oslo by train to Otta (4 h.), bus to Grotli ($3\frac{1}{2}$ h.), Djupvasshytta ($4\frac{1}{2}$ h.), Nordfjordeid (6 h.).

Driving from Bergen, the most direct way is to follow route 14, all the way to Volda and Ørsta for the western district (306 and 316 km.). This involves 3 to 4 short ferries; it is possible within a day. Or from Oslo follow the E6 to Otta (308 km.), then take route 15 through Ottadalen to Grotli (125 km.) or Djupvasshytta (146 km.) and on to Geiranger. Ferry to Hellesylt and lastly to Øye or Ørsta (39 or 64 km.).

BASES

Øye and the Union Hotel is a traditional base for ascents in the western district, but the nearby Patchellhytta is better placed for some local ascents, despite being small and without provisions. The small town of Ørsta has all facilities; combined with camping in Standalen or Bondalen, plus the use of a vehicle, much of the W can be covered easily.

MAPS

CAP 325M sh.2 Central Norway I covers the area and approaches. For detailed navigation and planning the modern 50M maps unfortunately do not show the crags and multiple tops too well.

1219 I	Stranda	1319 I	Romsdalen
1219 II	Geiranger	1319 II	Torsvatnet
1219 III	Hjørundfjord	1319 III	Tafjord
1219 IV	Sykkylven	1319 IV	Valldal

HUTS and other accommodation

Ålesund and Sunnmøre Turistforening operate all huts except for Torsbu which is DNT. Self-service and unstaffed huts use standard DNT keys.

Staffed huts:	beds	Map No.	4-fig. ref.
Kaldhusseter	42	1319 III	18-92
Reindalsseter	80	1319 III	26-96
Self-service huts: Pyttbua	34	1319 II	37-98
Torsbu	14	1319 II	40-88
Vakkerstøylen	24	1319 I	39-04
Veltdalsbu	12	1319 II	33-92

Unstaffed huts:	Fokhaugstova	40	1319 IV	10-22
	Patchellhytta	13	1219 II	81-00
	Velleseter	12	1219 IV	79-06

YH at Valldal.

WALKING TOURS

These are limited in scope and confined to the eastern district.

1. **Tafjord to Billingen** (3-4 days)
Tafjord – Reindalsseter – Veltdalsbu – Torsbu – Billingen. This tour can be continued S into the Breheimen (Area 7), firstly to Skridulaupbu.

2. **Billingen to Romsdal** (4 days)
Billingen – Torsbu – Pyttbua – Vakkerstøylen – Romsdal valley. This too can be continued by going a short way E in Romsdal, then into Dovre (Area 5), firstly to Aursjøhytta.

ASCENTS

SLOGJEN 1564m.
Or Slogen. 1st ascent 1870, John Klokk and brother (SE ridge).
   1a. SE ridge, normal route, marked footpath. From Øye take the Hellesylt road for about one km. to footpath going N. Follow steeply for 2km. to N, finally turning up SE ridge to summit. 8h. up and down.
   1b. SW face (Fjord route). Grade IV, sometimes moderate, sometimes difficult climbing. Go up the road towards Urke to a prominent gorge known as Armstrong-Vigdal. Follow L side until steep wall with chimney leading up L is reached. Follow this until overhanging section forces one out R to ridge. Go up ridge easily and into continuation of gorge for some 200m. Finally take easiest line on SW upper wall. In all, 8-10h. climbing.

KOLÅSTIND 1432m.
Slingsby called it the "Monarch of Sunnmøre". He climbed it in 1876 but failed to reach absolute top. 1st complete ascent 1880, A Hovden, N Kolas, Betzy Kjeldsberg (E flank).
   2. E flank, normal route, gl. and easy rock. From Standalshytta (ski hut) go N into Kvanndalen, then W up the Kolåstind gl. – some crevasses, usually easy, to rocky summit. About $3\frac{1}{2}$h. There are other interesting routes: E ridge, SW ridge, Kolåstind pinnacles (various up to grade IV).

SØRE SETRETIND 1358m.
   3. S pillar, III/IV. 1st ascent 1953, H Berg, J H Høye, R Øyen, O Simenstad. From Standalseter walk and scramble up steep hillside

JØNSHORN complex from SW

to platform at foot of central of 3 pillars. Work L, then more or less straight up for about 250m. (III,IV), mostly sound. Then loose and awkward scrambling to summit ridge with numerous pinnacles and tops. Go N along ridge, by-passing some pinnacles. There is a long abseil on E side down to a snow gully leading to gl. Or, continue N to very steep tower; descend, still going N with difficult climbing and abseils to gl. Easy descent E into Flatdalen. Very complex.

STORE SMØRSKREDTIND 1630m.
1st ascent 1884, W Eckroyd, W C Slingsby, John Klokk (E face).
 4. NE ridge, easy climbing. From Patchellhytta go SE and across small gl. to NE gap. Then up NE ridge, steep and loose in places, turning upper wall on L (6h.). This mountain has several technical routes: W ridge, NW ridge, SW face and ridge.

There are numerous other mountains with good walking and climbing ascents in this district. These include:

SKARTINDEN 1542m.
Long ridge with several tops and pinnacles S of Saebo. Shown on modern maps as Kvistad-kjerringane.
 5. E flank and S ridge, normal route, ungraded, scrambling with some climbing. From Skar on Hjørundfjorden first to Skarseter then by a small gl. to the S ridge, which is ascended to Søre Skartind(1433m.). One km. ridge traverse to main summit, probably moderate climbing.

BLÅTIND 1206m. 1182m.
 6. Double topped ridge at the W end of Bondalen. 1st ascent of both 1895, C W Patchell, J Simpson, from the gap. Ungraded, believed easy. From Kalvedalen in the N, via a gully to gap between the summits. Both peaks are reached easily.

JØNSHORN 1419m.
 7. Jønshornet. Long main ridge near seaward end of Hjørundfjorden with complexity of tops, pinnacles, side ridges and walls. Many routes of most grades. 1st ascent 1889, G Hastings by NE face. Normal way from Barstadvik, firstly up the valley and on to Rametinden (1198m.). Then NW ridge is followed for over one km. to main summit; scramble.

JAKTA 1588m.
 8. Lies immediately SW of Øye and has an enormous 1500m. W face rising from the fjord; no known route on this face. 1st ascent 1896, H C Bowen, C W Patchell by scrambling up the E ridge from Øye.
 Nearby Staven (1517m.) has a towering E face of about 1500m., dominating the Norangsdalen. No ascent of this face is known.

RÅNA 1586m.
Highest summit N of Urke on the E side of Hjørundfjorden. Several

minor gl. Great crags and ridges with towers and pinnacles. 1st ascent 1899, G Hastings, on the W side, exact route not known but described as "a mere scramble".

9. SE wall from Regndal gl. Ungraded snow/ice ascent and gl. crossing. From Urke via skar (col) between Grotdalstinden and Urkedalstind onto the heavily crevassed Regndal gl. This is followed for about 4km. to a gully SE of the top. Crossing the bergschrund can be awkward, but the ascent to the summit is believed easy, 6h. Return the same way, 4h. There are other routes up to grade IV: NE ridge, N wall, SW ridge.

Samer play-sledge and reindeer

Romsdal

WITHOUT exception this is the most famous rock climbing locality in Scandinavia. Great publicity has been given to its multi-day routes on the vertiginous walls of the main Romsdalen valley. The prospects for less ambitious but worthwhile climbing objectives are described below.

In common with all areas of the fjord region, the mountains are not high. The culminating point is Store Vengetind (1852m.), while the attractive Romsdalhorn (1550m.), Store Trolltind (1788m.) and others are lower still. Nevertheless they are often extremely savage and spectacular peaks, and with valleys nearly at sea level contribute to the feeling of great height.

No western area of Norway has reliable weather and Romsdal is no exception. Lengthy dry periods in summer, combined with long daylight hours, can produce superb climbing conditions. In a bad rainy summer many of the great wall routes never come into condition.

In the N, Langfjorden and Romsdalsfjorden act as a natural boundary; in the W the mountains merge into the Sunnmøre group; in the E, Lake Eikesdalen and its southern-reaching valley mark the division with Dovre; in the S the boundary is unclear – probably Ulvådalen to the Tafjord is a suitable line.

APPROACHES

By ship from Bergen; daily services along the coastal route to Ålesund (13h.) or Molde (18h.); bus links to Åndalsnes. By rail from Oslo to Dombås (5h.), change for Åndalsnes (1½h.). With a car, from Oslo follow E6 N to Dombås (355km.), then route 69 to Åndalsnes (103km.).

From Bergen the drive is a long, involved but scenic journey. The quickest way is to follow route 14, N over the ferries to Forde (171 km.), then on to Byrkjelo (64km.). From here, 2 possibilities. A low-level route to Ålesund on route 14, using 3 ferries (140km.), finally by the E69 to Åndalsnes (127km.). Or the high level scenic variation by route 60 to Stryn (60km.), route 15, then the tunnel link to join route 58, which is followed past Geiranger to Eidsdal (154km.); now a ferry to Linge, then route 63 over the spectacular Trollstigen pass to Åndalsnes (62km.).

ROMSDALSHORN from E

BASES

Compared with other Norwegian areas, Romsdal is small and compact, and therefore suitable for exploration from 1 or 2 centres. Åndalsnes is a natural focal point for the whole area and has every facility one would expect from a small town, including food shops, banks, garages, etc. From here roads can be taken to set up base camps without backpacking. Use upper Vengedal for the Vengetind - Romsdalhorn groups; upper Isterdal for the Trolltind - Kongen - Finnan group; Åndalsnes for the remainder.

MAPS

CAP 325M sh.2 Central Norway I shows the area and approaches from Bergen and Oslo. A Romsdalen special tourist sh. comes in the scale of 80M. Otherwise the area is covered by the modern SK 50M maps.

1319 I	Romsdalen	1319 IV	Valldal
1319 II	Torsvatnet	1320 II	Eresfjord
1319 III	Tafjord	1320 III	Åndalsnes

HUTS and other accommodation

Much of the Romsdal area is unsuitable for walking tours and huts will not be found. Suitable climbing bases exist in the valleys. Huts in the Isfjord group are owned by Molde and Romsdal Turistforening (MRT); in outlying mountains the huts are listed in Areas 8 and 10.

Self-service huts:	beds	Map No.	4-fig. ref.
Hoemsbu	36	1320 II	56–37
Masvassbu	22	1320 II	40–47
Unstaffed huts: Vasstindbu	6	1320 II	47–45
Svartvassbu	6	1320 II	51–41

WALKING TOUR

The area does not lend itself to the normal type of Scandinavian tour. Any extended tour involves travelling into other areas.

1. Romsdal to Dovrefjell (about 7 days)
Romsdal (Grøvdal) - Hoemsbu - Reinvassbu - Aursjøhytta - Grøvudalshytta - Åmotsdalshytta - Reinheim - Kongsvoll.

ASCENTS

In the main mountain groups within Romsdal there are virtually no walking ascents, although some summits in the little used western and southern districts are easily ascended.

VENGETIND ridges from W

Romsdal has acquired the reputation that it only suits the "hard" man; in fact there are a large number of climbs in the medium to lower grades. Other routes described as scrambling often involve uncertain rock in very exposed situations; these should be considered with caution by those less able or experienced.

STORE VENGETIND 1852m.
Venjetind. 1st ascent 1881, W C Slingsby, J Vigdal by NE flank.

1a. N ridge, the ordinary ascent/descent route, I/II. From Vengedal lake head across mountain flank then up easy snow gully to obvious gap in N ridge. Follow easiest line to summit, first on L then on R of ridge; the last few pitches are II.

1b. By ridge traverse from Søre Vengetind (1799m.) and Lille Vengetind (1820m.), II. Long traverse with fine situations on mainly excellent rock. From Hornvatnet go up directly and steeply towards Romsdalhorn, then traverse L (E) to Olaskar lake. Follow the broad S ridge of Søre V., pleasant scrambling (I/II) for some distance to its top (4-5h.). Go down to col with awkward scrambling in places and continue up S ridge of Lille V., exposed, short pitch of III. Descend to col, traverse over an obvious gallery to middle of E face of Store V., then its NE ridge (II) to summit (2-3h.). Descend by the N ridge.

ROMSDALHORN 1550m.
1st ascent believed to be 1828 by a peasant and a blacksmith, H Bjermeland, C Hoel. 1st "official" recorded ascent (after 6 attempts) by Carl Hall in 1881.

2. S ridge ordinary route, II. The classic ascent/descent involving much steep scrambling and some tricky route finding, despite the cairns. From Hornvatnet go straight up steeply to the cairned path and zigzags. These head L at first, then traverse back R to a steep section which can be climbed directly (III). More zigzags towards a big light coloured patch of rock (Den Gule Flekk), but not too high before traversing L into a large gully (Hall's Renne). Climb this keeping R to a steep exit wall, taken on the L (II+). Finally go up S ridge (exposed, II) to the summit (3-4h.).

STORE TROLLTIND 1788m.
Almost a roadside "crag", albeit 1600m. high. 1st ascent 1882 by the Dane Carl Hall with M Soggemoen, J Venge, ascending from Isterdalen.

3. W flank ordinary route, II-. From above the Stigfoss waterfalls follow path E round edge of the Isterdal valley, then ascend flank of the waterfall into the valley leading E towards Breidtind. Cairns go up snow slopes NE to a col W of Breidtind. Now an easy rising traverse under pinnacles of Klumpen and Stabben, then a mainly level cairned path to Brura Skar; impressive views. Continue the traverse under Brudgommen

KVANNDALSTIND from S

then ascend gullies (II) to Ugla Skar. Go through a hole in the ridge, traversing further W than the summit, using a gully system to reach the summit plateau. Finish up ridge E to summit (II+), 4h.

The complete Trolltind ridge has been of great significance in the history of Romsdal ascents. Other landmarks were the original E face route (IV-) in 1931 by Arne Randers-Heen, Erik Heen; E Pillar of the Trollryggen (1742m., VI-) in 1958 by Ralph Høibakk, A R Heen; N (Troll) Wall (Norwegian Route, VI+) in 1965 by L Pettersen, J Teigland, O D Enersen, O Eliassen; N face direct of Sondre Trolltind (1618m., VI+) in 1967 by R Baillie, J Amatt.

KONGEN 1614m.
1st ascent 1882, C Hall, M Soggemoen, E Norahagen, by SW face.

4. SW face ordinary route, ascent/descent, II-. From above the Stigfoss waterfalls go W up to Bispevatnet; follow the E bank and eventually attain col between Bispen and Kongen. Ascend the easy S ridge until it merges into the S wall. Head towards the summit, trending L across subsidiary ridges and up snowy gullies until close to summit, then move R up a rocky ridge (II) to summit (3h.).

In descent, start by following a cairned gully on the W face; leave it soon for a snowy gully further R. Now reverse ascent route to the S ridge, taking care not to go too far down the gullies (they end in steep slabs), 2h.

FINNAN 1786m.
1st ascent 1898, C Hall, M Soggemoen, E Norahagen, using SE ridge.

5. SE ridge, normal ascent/descent, II-. From above the Stigfoss waterfalls go W up to Bispevatnet; then cross to the W side and climb the ridge, broad at first. Follow this to Østre and Midtre Finnan, then a snow ridge to Sondre Finnan, possibly corniced. The actual SE ridge is finally followed to summit (3-4h.).

long-tailed skua

Nordmøre & Trollheimen

THE most northerly zone of the fjord ranges, though less well known than its Romsdal neighbour, is in some ways a more interesting area. In particular, rock climbing by Norwegians in the Innerdalen valley of the Nordmøre district is well developed. In Innerdalen and the nearby Sunndalen large walls closely rival those of Romsdal and scope remains for new and harder routes. The Trollheimen district affords excellent walking and ski-touring within a convenient framework of huts.

The highest summits in the eastern district (Trollheimen) are the Blåhø (1672m.) and Snota (1668m.). Further W, Nordmøre has steeper, higher and wilder mountains, some heavily glaciated, culminating in Store Trolla (1850m.) in Innerdalen, and Store Kalkjin (1880m.) in Sunndalen. The rock is mainly ancient gneiss, featuring large blocks and ledges.

The whole area, but especially Nordmøre, has a high reputation among Norwegians for its unspoilt scenic beauty and incidently the excellence of its salmon fishing. Certainly the Innerdalen valley is most attractive with unusually lush vegetation contrasting with magnificent rock walls and spires. A rewarding area for botanists, with an exceptionally high growth for some plants, eg giant nettles. This plant height is related to the distinctly maritime climate of cool summers and comparatively mild winters. The W parts receive very high precipitation and a great deal of cloud. June is probably the best month for a visit, although May has a stable reputation and S faces are normally clear then of snow.

The area is bordered in the N by route 65 from Skei through the Rindal valley; in the W by a series of fjords, sometimes known as the Nordmøre fjords; in the E by the major route E6 running N from Oppdal; in the S by the vague definition of route 16 from Oppdal and partly down the Sunndalen valley, but the high mountains S of Sunndalsøra should be included in the area.

APPROACHES

From Bergen by coastal ship (Hurtigruten) to Molde (18 h.) or Kristiansund (23 h.). Onward bus links to Sunndalsøra. From Oslo by train to Oppdal (5¼ h.); bus link to Sunndalsøra. Using your own transport, from Oslo follow the E6 northwards to Oppdal (435 km.), then take route 16 to Sunndalsøra (71 km.).

Driving from Bergen is a long and tiring journey. If no other options are available follow the access description given for Romsdal (Area 9), then take the coastal road following routes 64, 660 and finally 62 to Sunndalsøra (additional 137 km.).

BASES

Sunndalsøra (pop. 5000), heavily industrialised, is the main centre of the area with all normal facilities; food shops, bank, garages, etc.

For rock climbing, Innerdalen is easily reached by road from Sunndalsøra (c. 20 km.). Vehicles must be left at Nerdal, a possible base for the W mountains; poor and limited camping. Better bases higher in Innerdalen are reached on foot in 5 km. or more; 2 huts or camping.

For walking in Trollheimen there is practical backpacking to any point within the district. Starting points for walking tours include a number along route 16; Lønset for Bårdsgarden hut; Festa bridge for Gjevilvasshytta. Other starting points along routes 65 and E6.

MAPS

CAP 325M sh. 3 Central Norway II shows the overall area. Sheet 2 Central Norway I covers the approaches from Bergen and Oslo. There is a special tourist Trollheimen sh. at 80M. The SK 50M maps are:

1420 I	Snota	1420 IV	Stangvik
1420 II	Romfo	1520 III	Oppdal
1420 III	Sunndalsøra	1520 IV	Trollhetta

HUTS and other accommodation

All staffed huts are operated by Trondhjems Turistforening, who also own Bårdsgarden self-service hut. Kristiansund & Nordmøre Turistforening own Todalshytta.

Staffed huts:	beds	Map No.	4 fig. ref.
Gjevilvasshytta	54	1520 III	21-52
Jøldalshytta	48	1520 IV	26-70
Trollheimenshytta	55	1520 IV	12-66
Private staffed huts:			
Innerdalshytta	34	1420 II	88-54
Rendølssetra	30	1420 II	88-55
Self-service huts: Bårdsgarden	10	1420 II	07-50
Kårvatn Gard	19	1420 I	93-61
Unstaffed hut: Todalshytta	4	1420 IV	84-65

110

WALKING TOUR

Trollheimen Tour   (5-6 days)
Gjevilvasshytta - Jøldalshytta - Trollheimshytta - Kårvatn -
Innerdalshytta - Sunndalen.
   Shorter tours can be made through each district; a longer tour is to
continue into Dovre area.

ASCENTS   Nordmøre District - Innerdalen

STORE TROLLA   1850m.
   1. E face, ordinary route, I/II, ice axe useful. 1st ascent 1895 by
Klingenberg, Meisterlin. From Innerdalshytta follow the path S into
Giklingsdalen until past the lake. Cross inlet streams, heading W towards the E face, to start just S of the summit. The route follows a snow
gully for much of the way, breaking out L some distance before the NE
ridge, then crossing snow patches to the main ridge. This is climbed to
the summit, 6h.

SKARFJELL stortoppen   1790m.
   2. NW ridge, walk. 1st ascent 1850, J Holten, H Holthaug. From
Innerdalshytta follow the path into Giklingsdalen, crossing the outlet
stream before the lake (near the NTK hut). Traverse under the N wall
of Skarfjell towards the NW ridge, passing between the main face and
the Jutulene pinnacles. Ascend the broad ridge or NW flank to the top
(4 h.). An alternative start from Nerdal descends to the river (bridge)
and winds up through dense woodland and large boulders into Grasdalen.
Traverse across very rough, vegetated hillside to the Jutulene pinnacles.

   3. NE Tower, IV+. 1st ascent 1927, E Fjeld, J Innerdal. From
Innerdalshytta go up into Giklingsdalen, cross stream by NTK hut and
ascend grass/boulder slopes, $2\frac{1}{2}$ h. Then 4 climbing pitches for 200m.
plus 300m. scrambling/walking to summit, 3h. See diagram.

SKARFJELL midtoppen   1620m. (see diagram)
All the climbs below are approached as for no.3 above.
   4. Gunnbjørgs Route, V+, A2. 1st 1974, R Høibakk, O Leira.
Climb is 11 pitches, 300m. 9-12h.

   5. Premiediederet "Bugha", VI-. 1st 1976, B Hammeras, U G Hansen. First 5 pitches as for no.4 to a broad ledge. Then R and up a
prominent dièdre, free climbing. Total 9 pitches, 270m. 9-12h.

   6. Olavsveggen Direct, VI. 1st 1969, U G Hansen, H E Krabset.
   6a. Olavsveggen Direct, VI+, A2. 1st 1969, T Carlstrøm, H Hell-
strøm, E Holmgren. No.6 has 14 pitches (400m.); the first 5 are the
same as no.7. No.6a has 16 pitches (400m.), joining no.6 after the
first 7. Both routes, 6-8h.

SKARFJELL from E

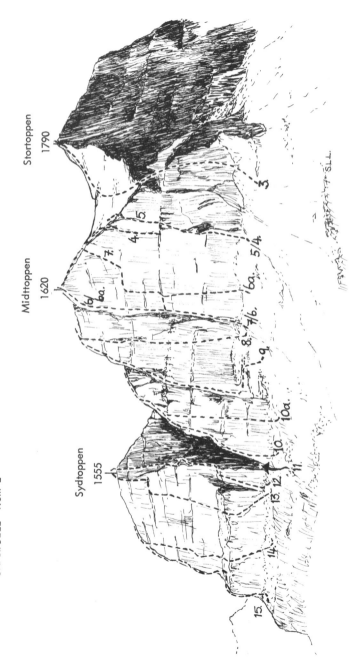

Stortoppen 1790

Midttoppen 1620

Sydtoppen 1555

7. Olavsveggen, VI-. 1st 1959, R Høibakk, A Mayr, F Horntnagel.
13 pitches, 350m. 5-8h.

8. Tordenpillar, VI-. 1st 1969, U G Hansen, I Walaas. 12 pitches,
350m. 7-10h.

9. Fugleggen, V-. 1st 1959, R Høibakk, A Mayr, F Horntnagel. 13
pitches, over 300m. 4-6h.

10. Mellomgjelveggen, IV. 1st 1958, P Vigerust, R LaPierre.
8 pitches, 250m., followed by scrambling, 3-5h.

10a. Mellomgjelveggen direct, V. 1st 1970, B Hammerås, O M
Sundnes. 7 pitches, 250m., joins no.10 for final scrambling. 3-5h.

11. Normal route, ungraded. Approach as for other routes to foot of
prominent snow gully. This is followed to top, then up gl.to the summit.
3-4h. from Innerdalshytta. Descent, $2\frac{1}{2}$h.

SKARFJELL sydtoppen 1555m.
All the climbs below are approached as for no.3 above.

12. Elinas Route Direct, V+. 1st 1965, Elina Platou, Einarsen,
R Høibakk. 11 pitches, 350m. 5-7h.

13. Betzys Route, VI-. 1st 1968, J Bruskeland, U G Hansen. 17
pitches, 350m. 7-9h.

14. Giklingveggen, V-. 1st 1960, R Høibakk, A Naess. 14 pitches,
350m. 5-7h.

15. South-East Tower, V. 1st 1955, L Arenz-Hansen, O Innerdal.
10 pitches, 300m. 3-5h.

STORE DALATÅRNET 1450m.
LITLE DALATÅRNET 1312m.
These 2 tops together make the famous tower of Innerdalen, now with a
network of climbs from I/II to V, and up to 500m. in length. 1st ascent
1889, E H Holten, J Nerdahl, G J Nygard, A O Rosset.

16. Store Dalatårnet by S face ordinary route (via Tarnskar), I/II.
From Innerdalshytta take the Giklingsdalen path to NE corner of the
lake. Now follow small path ascending E towards the prominent Tarnskar col. Go up a rocky step to a broad, slanting band which is taken
to the foot of the couloir leading to Tarnskar (often snowy). Climb
couloir, first on R side then on L, to the col. From here ascend the
ridge, exposed in places, first on L side, then on crest with pitches of
II to summit, 3h. Descend the same way.

17. Store Dalatårnet by W edge, III/IV. A harder but better climb.

From Innerdalshytta, as for no.16 to the broad, slanting band; continue up the normal couloir to another large band. Here traverse L to the ridge, which is followed more or less directly to the summit with pitches of II+/IV-/IV in about 200m. of climbing, 3-4h.

18. Litle Dalatårnet, W ridge, II/III. As for no.16/17 to the first band (known as Hoppet). Make a rising traverse L to the gully between Litle and Store summits. Climb pleasant rocky ridge on L to summit; pitches of II, III, 3h. Descend by same route; it is also possible to go down main couloir. Another variation is to ascend Store by NW ridge, IV+/V- for 175m.

DRONNINGSKRONA   1816m.

19. N ridge ordinary route, via Hestbreen gl. Ungraded. 1st ascent 1906, Slingsby, Sjølsvik. From Nerdal lake take the path into Grasdalen. Ford/wade the streams, heading W towards Hestbreen. On the gl. ascend obliquely to main ridge, keeping S of Hesten and Sandvikhaugen tops. Then follow ridge easily S for about 2km. to the summit, 3-4h. Descend the same way, or more directly by going down N for a few hundred m., then cutting NW down Grasdalsbreen.

wolf

D. CENTRAL BORDER
HIGHLANDS

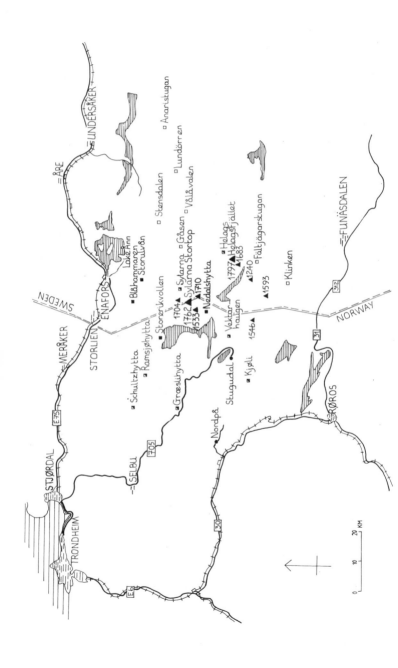

Sylene - Sylarna group

THE most southerly part of a long, virtually unbroken chain of mountains stretching N along the Norwegian/Swedish border for over 800
km. The border highlands continue further S in the form of hilly moor-
land and finally lower forested hills, mostly about 1000m. in height or
less. This is not a significant upland area; nevertheless it offers some
worthwhile walking and skiing.

Sylarna is a huge massif, almost 7750 sq. km. in extent, much of which
is occupied by a vast upland plateau. Extensive sections lie above
1200m. with scattered and isolated mountains rising to almost 1800m.
The highest summit, Helagsfjället (1797m.), is entirely in Sweden; the
second peak, Sylarna, stands along the border, but its highest point
Stortop (1762m.) lies in Norway. These 2 and other prominent tops are
composed of resistant gabbro. Small gl. exist on the Swedish side of
the range and are the most southerly in Sweden.

The area is noted for its rich and varied wildlife, although the most
outstanding location (Lake Ånn) at 525m. is found on the limits of the
mountain and lowland. Over 100 species of birds breed on and immediately around Lake Ånn. Elk, reindeer, wolverine and lynx inhabit
the area and there is a fine selection of birds of prey.

Scrambling and climbing possibilities are outweighed by better touring,
both on foot and ski. The Swedish side in particular attracts tourers
from Stockholm and further afield, while the Norwegian side is mainly
used by people from the Trondheim area.

In the N the area is bordered by the E75 highway from Trondheim to
Östersund through the important pass at Storlien; in the S, by route 31
in Norway, continuing in Sweden as route 312; in the E an outlier of
the mountains reaches to Lake Storsjön, effectively forming the boundary; the W boundary is not well defined and approximates to lower
hills lying immediately E of the E6 highway.

APPROACHES

From Oslo by train to Trondheim ($8\frac{1}{2}$ h.). Bus links to the Norwegian
(Sylene) districts. From Oslo, alternatively by rail via Røros ($6\frac{1}{2}$ h.).
Onward buses or taxi. From Gothenburg by train to Oslo is a poor
link (5 h.). Onward train to Trondheim/Røros, etc.

Similarly, from Gothenburg by train through Sweden to Storlien (or other starting points) via Gävle (16½ h.). From Stockholm to Storlien (11 h.). By car from Oslo, take the E6 N to Trondheim (557 km.), the E75 to the border at Storlien (105 km.), or other nearby starting points. Alternatively go via Lillehammer and Messelt to Røros (429 km.).

Driving through Sweden or Norway from Gothenburg is long and not particularly recommended because Swedish Rail provide a convenient and rapid - though fairly expensive - link.

STARTING POINTS AND BASES

Essentially a touring area, there are no ideal bases for exploring the whole area. Starting possibilities are numerous; points can easily be worked out from the hut locations and a regional touring map.

MAPS

CAP 325M sh.3 Central Norway II shows the whole area and the approaches through Norway. LB 400M sh.6 Södra Norrland depicts the Swedish side of the group and the approaches through Sweden. The LB 100M New Mountain Series gives excellent detail of all the Swedish and part of the Norwegian side: Z6 Storlien - Vålådalen - Ljungdalen; Z7 Åre - Bydalen - Hallen; Z8 Helags - Funäsdalen - Rogen.

LB also produce special sheets in 50M: Storlien; Åre; Oviksfjallet; Tännäs - Rogen - Grövelsjön; Funäsdalen - Fjällnäs.

The Norwegian side is covered by SK 50M official survey maps:

1720 I	Stugusjø	1721 II	Essandsjøen
1720 IV	Ålen	1721 III	Tydal
1721 I	Meråker	1721 IV	Flornes

HUTS and other accommodation:

Huts on the Norwegian side are owned or operated by Trondhjems Turistforening, Hans Hagerupsgt.1, 7000 Trondheim. Huts on the Swedish side are owned by the Swedish Touring Club (STF).

	Norway		
Staffed huts:	beds	Map No.	4 fig. ref.
Nordpå	35	1720 IV	15–82
Nedalshytta	68	1720 I	53–86
Storerikvollen	65	1721 II	50–01
Self-service huts:			
Graeslihytta	10	1721 III	24–98
Kjøli	8	1720 IV	33–73
Ramsjøhytta	24	1721 II	37–06

Self-service huts:	beds	Map No.	4-fig. ref.
Schultzhytta	30	1721 III	26-11
Vektarhaugen	6	1720 I	49-79
Private hut: Stugudal	20	1720 I	46-77

	Sweden		
Staffed huts: Blåhammaren	46	Z6	12.11E/63.12N
Storulvån	90	Z6	12.22E/63.11N
Self-service huts:			
Ånarisstugan	10	Z7	13.20E/63.06N
Fältjägarstugan	20	Z8	12.26E/62.49N
Gåsen	52	Z6	12.33E/63.03N
Helags	72	Z6	12.31E/62.55N
Klinken	18	Z8	12.18E/62.43N
Lunndörren	30	Z7	13.03E/63.04N
Stensdalen	38	Z6	12.44E/63.07N
Sylarna	90	Z6	12.17E/63.03N
Vålåvalen	20	Z6	12.48E/63.02N

WALKING TOURS

Among many possible walking or ski tours in the area, 2 are as follows:

1. Sylene Tour (7-8 days)
Nordpå - Graeslihytta - Schultzhytta - Ramsjøhytta - Storerikvollen - Nedalshytta - Stugudal - Kjøli - Nordpå.

2. Sylarna Tour (10 days)
Vålådalen - Stensdalen - Gåsen - Sylarna - Blåhammaren - Storerikvollen (N) - Nedalen (N) - Helags - Vålåvalen - Lunndörren - Vålådalen. (N = Norway)

ASCENTS

SYLARNA Stortop 1762m.
   1. W face and N ridge, a strenuous walk. From Nedalshytta take the marked path N towards Sylarna hut. After about 5km. a subsidiary path swings E, up to the tarn known as Syltjärna (1034m.). From here ascend steeply towards the main ridge, grassy at first, then taking an ascending traverse SE to join the main ridge between the Stortop and Lilletop. Follow ridge S to summit, 6-7h.

   2. NE face and N ridge, a walk. From Sylarna hut descend NW to river Sylälven. Cross bridge then head W at first towards Vaktklumpen, finally SW to ridge between Stortop and Lilletop. Follow ridge S to summit, 4-5 h.

HELAGSFJÄLLET 1797m.

3. SE face, a walk. From Helags hut take the path S towards Fält-jägarstugan, to a point near the reindeer fence. Ascend fairly steeply, roughly following the fence line to reach a broad ridge. Go W then NW along a narrower ridge to summit, 4h.

red deer

Børgefjell & Swedish Västerbotten·
N. Jämtland

THE most southerly of the truly northern mountain groups, this vast area
has a wilderness atmosphere and is very little visited. Even the Norwegians and Swedes confine themselves to a few more popular locations.
It is a fairly difficult zone to define, and is to some extent a composite of several mountain areas. Within its boundaries are 2 National
Parks; Børgefjell in Norway and Pieljekaise in Sweden; also in Sweden the huge Vindelfjällen Nature Reserve.

Spanning virtually $3\frac{1}{2}$ degrees of latitude and with a maximum breadth
of about 130 km., the overall area is more than 12,000 sq. mi. (larger
than Wales), though part of this includes forested valleys and lakes.
Only a few roads run from W to E and cross the frontier.

While not a significant area for mountaineers it undoubtedly should
appeal strongly to wilderness travellers, having few huts and virtually
no other accommodation. Camping is almost unrestricted, the wildlife
is rich and fascinating, there is good fishing and few people. Comp-
etence and a degree of self-sufficiency are required to cope with its
great rivers and vast open spaces.

The Norwegian Børgefjell Park only forms about 2000 sq. km. but typi-
fies the area, having great tracts of heathland and a varied flora and
fauna. Mammals include mountain hare, arctic fox, elk and reindeer,
even the occasional lynx, wolverine, wolf and bear. Wading birds are
numerous including red-necked phalarope in the wetter parts, with the
rough-legged buzzard and an occasional golden eagle or snowy owl to
be found over the heaths and mountains.

The Swedish Vindelfjällen Reserve is larger (over 4000 sq. km.) and
more varied in its landscape, flora and fauna. The district around
Ammarnäs is particularly famous, with more than 200 bird species having been recorded. Pieljekaise Park is much smaller (150 sq. km.) and
contains unspoiled mountain birch forest.

In the W, the E6 highway forms an obvious area boundary as far as its
junction with route 73; in the N, firstly route 73 to the frontier – the
continuation following this N, then E along route 375 (Sweden) as far as

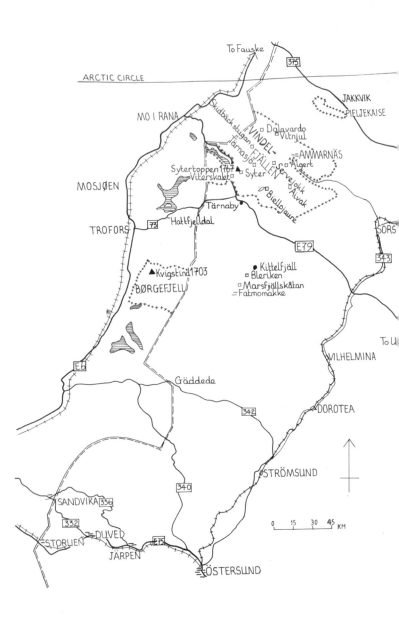

Jäkkvik; in the E, broken isolated fells make it impractical to define exactly; in the S, the E75 through the pass at Storlien is definitive.

APPROACHES

From Oslo by train to Trondheim ($8\frac{1}{2}$ h.). By train again (or bus) E to Storlien (3 h.) for access to the extreme S of the area. To reach the far N of the zone, take the train N from Trondheim to various points, eg. Trofors or Mosjøen (6 h.); Mo i Rana (7 h.); Lonsdal on the Arctic Circle (8 h.). A few bus links or taxis can then be taken to a choice of starting points. From Gothenburg or Stockholm by rail to Östersund in $12\frac{1}{2}$ h. or $7\frac{1}{2}$ h., then by the narrow gauge inland line through Strömsund (2 h.), Dorotea ($3\frac{1}{2}$ h.), Vilhelmina ($4\frac{1}{2}$ h.), Sorsele ($7\frac{1}{2}$ h.). Finally by buses or taxis to possible starting points.

With a car from Oslo, follow the E6 to Trondheim (557 km.), then on to Trofors or Båfjellmo (367 km.). From here route 73 to Hattfjelldal (34 km.) - a useful junction for several starting points in the northern Norwegian part of the area.

From Gothenburg it is possible to drive on the E3 to Örebro, then E18 and route 55 to Uppsala (560 km.). Afterwards go N on the E4 as far as Sundsvall, then 4 important roads lead off W into the mountains. E75 through to Östersund and Storlien (560 km. and 670 km.); subsidiary routes 336 and 332 leave the E75 at Järpen and near Duved, both to cross the frontier at Sandvika (about 720 km.). Further N another subsidiary route 340 crosses into Norway, N of Hotagen. Route 342 goes to the border near Gaddede (789 km.). For the most northern districts continue on the E4 to Umeå, then on the E79 through to Tärnaby (over 900 km.). From the E79, route 343 can be taken to Sorsele and eventually to Ammarnäs. The most northerly part of all is reached along route 375, known as "Silvervägen", to Jäkkvik and the frontier.

STARTING POINTS AND BASES

The area is best suited for backpacking and there are no proper bases for overall exploration of such a huge zone. Tärnaby and Ammarnäs both make good bases for exploration of their surrounding districts.

Starting points are numerous. Storlien in the S, Hattfjelldal in the N, are particularly convenient; the E6 road and the railway flank the W side of the area to give many potential starting points. On the Swedish side Kittelfjall has a YH where a marked trail begins. Tärnaby is probably the largest and best developed community, for the extreme NE of the area. Ammarnäs is on the Kungsleden long distance footpath, as is Jäkkvik in the far N of the area.

MAPS

CAP 325M sh.3 Central Norway II covers approaches and most of the southern sections of this area, in both Norway and Sweden. CAP 400M sh.4 Central Norway III shows the Norwegian approaches to the northern sections and covers the mountains on both sides of the border. LB 400M sh.7 Mellersta Norrland is better for the Swedish approaches.

In SK 50M for the Norwegian side, several sheets overlap the border into Sweden. Where this occurs SK often, but not always, leaves the Swedish side virtually blank.

1722 II	Vuku	1924 III	Tunnsjøen
1822 III	Bellingen	1924 IV	Røyrvik
1822 IV	Vera	1925 I	Susendal
1823 II	Gjevsjøen	1925 II	Børgefjell
1823 III	Snåsa	1925 III	Majavatn
1923 I	Murusjøen	1925 IV	Svenningdal
1923 II	Sørli	1926 II	Hattfjelldal
1923 III	Blåfjellhatten	2025 III	Ranseren
1923 IV	Nordli	2025 IV	Skarmodal
1924 I	Jomafjellet	2026 III	Krutfjell
1924 II	Limingen		

The Swedish side is covered by the LB 100M Nya Fjallkartan series with superimposed information including routes, huts, etc.

BD15	Nasafjöll - Vuoggatjålme - Ammarfjöllet
BD16	Vuoggatjålme - Pieljekaise - Ammarnäs
AC 1	Umbukta - Artfjället - Tärnaby
AC 2	Hemavan - Norra Storfjället - Gardsjön
AC 3	Tärnaby - Södra Storfjället - Skalmodal
AC 4	Skalmodal - Fjällfjällen - Stekenjokk
AC 5	Virisen - Marsfjället - Saxnäs
Z 1	Stekenjokk - St. Blåsjön - Frostviken
Z 2	Klimpfjället - Saxnäs - Sjoutnäset
Z 3	Frostviken - Hotagsfjällen - Valsjöbyn
Z 4	Skäckerfjallën - Kall
Z 5	Hotagen - Mjölkvattnet - Kall

HUTS and other accommodation

There is no comprehensive hut chain, except along the Kungsleden and in Vindelfjällen. In addition there are scattered huts and reindeer herders shelters on both sides of the border, all privately owned, and few of these can be used. Details of the current situation is best obtained from DNT or STF head offices.

The area is ideally suited for camping. For long cross country journeys self-sufficiency is essential, although it should be practical to arrange tours to include an occasional deviation to the nearest settlement for provisions, etc.

STF huts in Vindelfjällen:

Aigert	22 beds	map AC 2	16.06E/65.57N
Servejokk	30	AC 2	15.46E/65.58N
Syter	30	AC 1	15.24E/65.53N
Tärnasjö	30	AC 1	15.30E/65.59N
Viterskalet	16	AC 1	15.11E/65.53N

Private huts (locked):

Aivak	4	AC 2	16.07E/65.48N
Biellojaure	4	AC 2	15.41E/65.48N
Dalavardo	4	BD15	15.39E/66.12N
Skidbäcksstugan	6	BD15	15.32E/66.05N
Vitnjul	4	BD15	16.01E/66.09N

2 huts are found on the short marked trail from Kittelfjall to Fatmomakke.

Bleriken	16	AC 5	15.22E/65.11N
Marsfjällskåtan	4	AC 5	15.16E/65.06N

WALKING ROUTES AND ASCENTS

Outside of Vindelfjällen marked paths rarely occur and few route descriptions exist in either Norwegian or Swedish. In this wild, pioneering locale many possibilities for touring can be devised using your own ideas, map and compass.

The highest summit in the area lies in the Swedish Norra Storfjället - Sytertoppen (1767m.). This group holds a number of interesting looking peaks, probably with good walking or scrambling ascents. The highest summit in the Norwegian sector is Kvigstind (1703m.), in the Børgefjell National Park - no route details, but as with other mountains of the area it appears to be walking without technical difficulties.

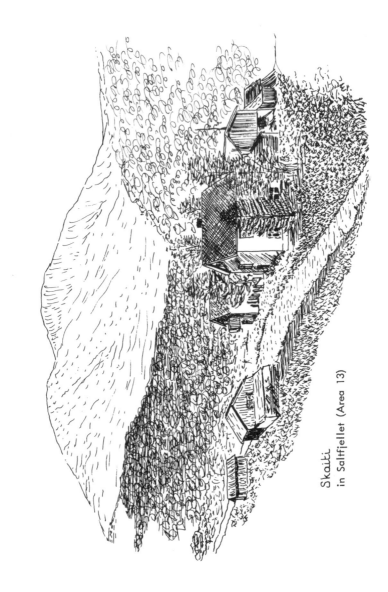

Skaiti
in Saltfjellet (Area 13)

E. ARCTIC NORWAY

Svartisen - Saltfjellet - Okstindan - Beiarn

ALTHOUGH this area actually consists of 4 separate mountain and gl. groups, they are sufficiently close geographically to be conveniently included together. It is a zone characterised by ice-caps, both large and of a remnant type, all steadily declining in size until about 1970; since then there has been some local moderate growth. The largest by far is Svartisen, at 369 sq. km. the second largest in Norway – though strictly speaking it is in 2 parts. Okstindan (46 sq. km., slightly S of the Arctic Circle) is the next largest in the area, with numerous smaller remnant ice-caps dotted about everywhere. In Beiarn one attains 12 sq.km.

Okstindan, Svartisen and Beiarn groups all have some climbing routes and potential for further development. Saltfjellet is mainly a touring district with an established hut system. The highest summit of the area, Oksskolten (1915m), lies in the Okstindan group and is also the highest summit in northern Norway. In the W sector of Svartisen, Snøtinden (1594m.), and in the E sector, Sniptinden (1591m.), are the highest points. Ølfjallet (1751m.) is the highest top in Saltfjellet, and Høgtinden (1405m.) the highest in the Beiarn group.

The overall area is effectively bordered in the W by the much indented coastline; in the S by the E6 road running eastwards, then route 73 to the Swedish border; in the E by the Swedish border; and in the N by the long Saltfjorden and the road E to Sulitjelma.

APPROACHES

The coastal express ship (Hurtigruten) arrives daily from Bergen to Sandnessjøen (53h.), or to Bodø (61h.). Onward links by local ferries or buses. By rail from Oslo to Mo i Rana (15½h.), or Fauske (18½h.). By car, for Okstindan take the E6 from Oslo as far as Korgen (1022 km.), then minor route 806 to the S and later E, finally by small tracks.

For Svartisen take the E6 past Mo i Rana to Rossvoll (1075km.), then N and NW by small roads and tracks. For Saltfjellet continue further along the E6 to the head of Dunderlandsdalen (1115km.), and a choice of starting points directly from the E6 as it runs N.

For the Beiarn ranges take the E6 as far N as Medby (1221 km.), followed by minor route 812, going W into the district. Alternatively some of the N summits can best be reached by local ferry from the Bodø to Fauske road (route 80).

STARTING POINTS AND BASES

The compact Okstindan group can easily be explored from a choice of camp bases round its perimeter. Mo i Rana is the nearest medium size town, with all necessary facilities.

Svartisen has very limited road access; bases near to the S roadheads have been used and it should be possible to use the western fjord approaches to find a base for the W sector of the ice-cap. Mo i Rana is the nearest town to the E sector, Glomfjord nearest to the W sector.

Saltfjellet is a large, more widespread district, equipped with touring huts, and has good road access to many parts.

There is minor road access into several parts of the Beiarn ranges and numerous local buses can be used.

MAPS

CAP 400M sh. 4 Central Norway III shows the whole area moderately well and the approaches clearly. The 50M survey maps have recently been revised and the whole area is now covered by modern maps.

Okstindan:	1926 I	Rosvatnet	2026 IV	Hjartfjell
	1927 II	Korgen	2027 III	Store Akersvandet
Svartisen:	1927 I	Mo i Rana	1928 III	Melfjord
	1927 IV	Sjona	2028 III	Blakkådal
Saltfjellet:	2027 IV	Storforshei	2128 II	Graddis
	2028 II	Bjøllådal	2128 III	Lønsdal
	2128 I	Balvatnet	2128 IV	Junkerdal
Beiarn:	1928 I	Glomfjord	2029 II	Misvaer
	2028 I	Beiardalen	2029 III	Saltstraumen
	2028 IV	Arstaddalen		

HUTS and other accommodation

Okstindan: unstaffed huts run by Hemnes Turistforening, 8646 Korgen.

	beds	Map No.	4-fig. ref.
Kjendsvasshytta	30	2027 III	66-27
Gråfjellhytta	8	1926 I	57-19
Steinbua	3	1927 II	59-21
Leirbotnhytta	8	1927 II	60-22

Svartisen : Unstaffed huts are run by Rana Turistforening. Keys and
booking : Rana Turistkontor, Strandgata, Boks 225, 8601 Mo i Rana.

Blakkådalshytta	12	2028 III	73-81
Kvitsteindaltunet	10	2027 II	02-40
Sauvasshytta	4	2027 II	88-41
Svartisdalshytta	6	2027 IV	65-73
Virvasshytta	6	2127 IV	16-54

Saltfjellet and Beiarn : All huts are unstaffed and usually locked. Huts
are run by Bodø og Omegns Turistforening (BOT), Storgt.30, 8000 Bodø.
Also by Sulitjelma Turistforening (ST).

Argaladhytta (BOT)	3	2128 I	34-14
Balvasshytta (ST)	4	2128 I	38-23
Beiarstua (BOT)	14	2028 IV	86-15
Bjellavasstua (BOT)	20	2028 I	02-14
Krukkistua (BOT)	12	2028 II	02-95
Ljøsenhammerstua (BOT)	9	2029 II	06-35
Lurfjellhytta (BOT)	10	2029 II	89-45
Lønsstua (BOT)	18	2128 III	20-02
Midtistua (BOT)	16	2028 I	00-04
Saltfjellstua (BOT)	8	2028 II	01-99
Skaiti (Trygvebu) (BOT)	16	2128 IV	30-09
Tjorvihytta (ST)	10	2128 I	42-31

WALKING TOURS

1. Umbukta to Korgen, Okstindan (4 days)
Umbukta - Kjennvasshytta - Leirbotnhytta - Gråfjellhytta - Inderdalen.

2. Bjøllånes to Medby, Saltfjellet (5 days)
Bjøllånes - Krukkistua - Midtistua - Bjellåvasstua - Ljøsenhammerstua -
Medby.

3. Lønsdal to Sulitjelma, Saltfjellet (4-5 days)
Lønsdal - Skaiti (Trygvebu) - Argaladhytta - Balvasshytta (Skiei'dihytta)
- Tjorvihytta - Sulitjelma.

ASCENTS

While it is known that climbs exist on all important summits within the
region, full details and accurate gradings do not appear to be available.
Included below are outlines for various summits with known routes.

131

OKSSKOLTEN 1915m.

1st ascent 1900, P Stordal, route not known.

    1. NW ridge, ungraded. 1st ascent 1900, K Bing, P K Fjelldal, K P Krokan. From Kjenvasshytta go S and cross the Okstindbreen gl., crevasses probable. Ascend NW ridge rather indirectly up steep boulder fields and slabs to summit, believed mainly scrambling, 5h. Go down the same way, 4h.

    2. Fine looking SE ridge from Oxcol is believed to offer climbing up to grade IV.

OKSHORN 1907m.

1st ascent 1900, K Bing, A Bonta by NW ridge.

    3. W face and NW ridge from Oxcol, ungraded but possibly III. Approached up heavily crevassed gl. to Oxcol, sometimes 2 bergschrunds. Ascend ridge, very narrow in places and some exposed climbing. Descend the same way or traverse S ridge to Svartfjell.

SVARTFJELL 1866m.

    4. NE face, I/II. Go up gl. towards Svartfjell, crossing bergschrund. Ascend steep slabs and chimneys of NE face to summit, giving 3h. of climbing. Easy descent by S ridge to gl. flank.

    5. E ridge, III/IV. 1963, R M Gamble, F L Jenkins. From a camp S of Lake 748m. route goes eastwards up gl., then southwards to snow col on E ridge. Alpine style ridge of 275m., III, possibly IV, to top.

AUSTRE SVARTFJELL 1602m.

1st ascent, A Hoel and party by E ridge, then believed to have taken W ridge to Svartfjell before descending easily to W.

STEIKVASSTIND 1741m.

1st ascent 1908, A Hoel and party by NW ridge, and down S ridge.

Immediately S of Kjendsvasshytta the Okskalvene ridge runs N-S with 3 distinct peaks.

NORDRE OKSKALV 1591m.

1st ascent 1908, A Hoel, P K Fjelldal by steep W face. Same party also ascended Midtre Okskalv (1509m.) and traversed to Søre Okskalv. Søre Okskalv (1676m.), 1st ascent 1883, C Rabot, P K Krokan, route not known.

OKSTIND 1803m.

1st ascent 1860, A O Brygfjelldal and son, route not known.

    6. SE ridge, probably I/II. Gained from its eastern snowfield. The ridge gives good scrambling and easy climbing, about 5h.

VESTRE TVILLINGTIND 1830m.
1st ascent 1900, V H Gatty, J Vigdal, E Hande, route not known.
  7. E face and ridge, I/II, possibly III. Gained from central snowfield, mainly scrambling, hardest section thought to be close to top.

VESSTIND 1724m.
1st ascent 1900, V H Gatty and party using a snow ridge on E face.

Svartisen

Most tops are of the nunatak type and all appear to have been ascended.
The first thorough exploration of Svartisen ice-cap was made by Charles
Rabot (French) in 1882. A variety of traverses have been made on foot
and by ski across both the western and eastern sectors.

SNØTINDEN 1599m.
Culminating point of the ice-cap, in its western sector. Believed to be
best ascended from Vesterdalen, but no details.

SNIPTINDEN 1591m.
Highest point of the eastern sector.
  1. S ridge, scrambling and gl. crossing; rope, crampons and ice axe
recommended. From a camp or the road in Svartisdalen follow the track
along N shore of Svartisvatnet (boat sometimes available).   Continue
on rising track, then past Austerdalsisen gl. tongue to camping place at
W end of lake (Austerdalsvatnet). Head N, crossing river where it can
be forded at a tributary stream; follow this to a gully. Ascend to W of
falls and follow river up to basin under upper falls coming down from
Kamplivatnet. Scramble E up cliff into Kamplivatnet cirque, then up
to col on N arm of cirque. More scrambling using rocky benches to
snowline and to pt.1392m. Head NE across icecap to foot of SE ridge
of Kamptinden (1534m.). Cross bergschrund and contour to the end of
S ridge of Sniptinden, scrambling up this to summit. $5\frac{1}{2}$ h. from the
Austerdalsvatnet.

BLAKKÅTINDEN 1300m.
  2. SW flank. Scrambling and gl. crossing; rope, crampons and axe.
From Svartisdalen, as for no.1 to junction in path before gl. tongue.
Go R, scrambling up benches and ledges to cairn at 702m. Continue
up ridge to further cairns at 1136m. and 1225m. Follow ice-cap fringe
to summit, 5h.

ISTINDEN 1572m.
  3. Long gl. crossing, rope, axe, crampons. From Svartisdalen go
N to Brunvatnet lakes (campsite). Head W over Gabrok (1098m.), to

cross ice-cap finger to Blåkkåtind SE ridge; follow this to latter summit. Now go across main ice-cap on 010 bearing, following E edge of ice with some crevasses to rocks of Bloksberg (1310m.). Continue N for about 4km. then NW to the summit rocks; crevasses possible. 7h. from Brunvatnet.

There are a number of neighbouring mountains which have been ascended and also offer further scope for routes.

Beiarn

The Beiartinder group is situated SW of Beiarfjorden. The most westerly peak, Stortind (1329m), is reputedly difficult.

Vestre Småtind (1148m.). 1st ascent 1920, N B Grondahl, E Quale, F Schelderup. Ascended from the E with some exposed climbing, grade not known. Austre Småtind (1320m.) and Midtre Småtind (1225m.), 1st by same party the following day; by a traverse from E gap to Midtre & Vestre summits.

The Børvasstinder group forms a distinctive backdrop from Bodø and consists of 2 parallel ridges. The rock is mainly loose slate.

Åseltinder (highest top 1176m.). A ridge with 5 tops; all have separate routes, of which little is known. 1st ascent of pt.1046m. was in 1885 by O Aanderud, grade not known.

Falkflagtinder (highest top 1143m.). A ridge with 6 tops. All have been ascended separately and a complete traverse has been made. 1st ascent 1888 by O Aanderud.

A little further S, Beiardalen valley is bounded on the W and S by a number of higher and potentially interesting peaks and medium size gl. The highest is Stormyrtinden (1546m.). No route details available.

Saltfjellet

The best known mountain is Solvågtind (1561m.), which rises E of the E6 road. Quite spectacular, there is an ascent by the E face.

white-tailed eagle

Sulitjelma/Blåmannsisen - Tysfjord - Narvik

A LARGE, composite area mainly forming the border with Sweden. It effectively includes 3 different groups and this wildly beautiful zone reveals Norway at its narrowest; the distance between the head of Hellemofjorden and the Swedish border is less than 16km.

Ice-caps feature strongly; Blåmannsisen is the 5th largest in Norway (87 sq. km.); Sulitjelma or Salajekna (33sq. km., partly in Sweden); Giccečakka, 13th (25 sq. km.); Frostisen, 14th (25 sq. km.); Storsteinsfjellbreen (12 sq. km.); plus numerous minor ones. The highest summits are the nunataks of the Sulitjelma group; Suliskongen at 1907m. while 2 other tops exceed 1800m. In the N, the highest summit of the Storsteinfjellet reaches 1893m. In the intervening 140km. there are scores of little known and little used mountains.

The overall area is bordered in the S by the Sulitjelma massif and the valley from Sulitjelma town to Fauske and the sea; in the E by the Swedish border, although Swedish Sulitelma will be included here; in the W by the deeply indented and dramatic coastline; in the N the border is difficult to define, but the border of Nordland and Troms provinces could be applied.

APPROACHES

The coastal express ship (Hurtigruten) gives access only to the extreme S of the area, arriving daily at Bodø from Bergen in 61h. Rail access only to the extreme S at Fauske ($18\frac{1}{2}$h. from Oslo); for the northern districts, rail Gothenburg to Narvik in 26h. The Nord-Norge bus runs from Fauske to Narvik (5h.) twice daily June to August - useful but a limited number of stopping places. By car, follow the E6 from Oslo to Fauske (1246km.) through numerous possible starting points to Narvik (1475km.)

STARTING POINTS AND BASES

Sulitjelma/Blåmannsisen can be explored from camping bases; reprovisioning from Sulitjelma town which has road access from Fauske. Tysfjord is mainly very remote; some parts require local or rented boat

access; numerous camping bases possible but self-sufficiency essential.
Narvik has all necessary facilities and is close to some mountains. Just
S of Narvik the Skjomdalen valley provides a good starting point for
the Storsteinfjellet and other mountains.

MAPS

CAP 400M sh.4 Central Norway III shows the whole area and the approaches well. Most of the SK50M maps are recent; the remainder are
being revised and should be completed by 1988.

1331 I	Skjomen	2030 II	Kjerringøy
1331 II	Frostisen	2129 I	Sisovatn
1331 III	Kjøpsvik	2129 II	Sulitjelma
1331 IV	Evenes	2130 I	Sagfjorden
1431 I	Bjørnfjell	2130 II	Gjerdal
1431 II	Čunojávri	2130 III	Helldalisen
1431 III	Skjomdalen	2130 IV	Nordfjold
1431 IV	Narvik	2229 III	Låmivatnet
1432 III	Gratangen	2230 I	Bjørntoppen
2029 I	Valnesfjord	2230 III	Linnajavrre
2029 IV	Bodø	2230 IV	Hellemobotn

For the Swedish side of Sulitelma, LB 100M Nya Fjällkartan sh.BD12
Staloluokta-Sulitelma-Kvikkjokk.

HUTS and other accommodation

Sulitjelma Touring Club (ST) own 5 unstaffed huts, always locked and
keys only from secretary in Sulitjelma.

Muorkihytta	13 beds	map 2229 III	ref. 59-38
Ny-Sulitjelma	20	2129 II	49-47
Sorjoshytta	8	2229 III	54-55

There are 2 unstaffed huts on the Swedish side; no cookers and little
equipment.

Staddajokk	12	BD 12	16.29E/67.14N
Sårjåsjaure	14	BD 12	16.35E/67.15N

Narvik Touring Club (NOT) own 6 unstaffed huts, normally all locked.
Key from Narvik Rådhus (town hall).

Cainhavaggehytta	12	1431 III	22-59
Cunojavrrehytta	12	1431 II	79-67
Gautelishytta	12	1431 III	18-50
Hunddalshytta	18	1431 IV	19-81
Losihytta	8	1431 III	15-66

YH in Narvik.

WALKING TOURS

The Sulitjelma area huts will allow a short 3-4 day tour round the main mountain massif. This can be extended by continuing S into Saltfjellet; alternatively continue E to join the Swedish hut system. In the Narvik area, one suggested route:

Katterat railway station – Skjomen   (5-6 days)
Katterat – Hunddalshytta – Losihytta – Cunojavrrehytta – Cainhavarre-hytta – Gautelishytta – Skjomen. This tour can be extended several days by going E into Sweden from Cunojavrrehytta, returning by linking up with Gautelishytta.

Alternatively, starting at Skjomen a tour can be extended beyond the railway at Katterat, N on to the Troms border trail.

Although there are no huts in the Tysfjord area there are a few mark-ed and cairned trails, mainly running W-E and joining up with the Sw-edish system.

ASCENTS
Sulitjelma / Blåmannsisen

Sulitjelma (Norway), Sulitelma (Sweden). A complex ice-cap massif; the main gl. is Sallajiekna and is roughly encircled by several distinct nunatak tops. Frequent cloud cover over large expanses of gl. and snow makes good navigation essential in this district.

SULISKONGEN 1907m.
1a. The highest top. E face and SE gl. approach. Grade I/II. 1st ascent 1900, V H Gatty, J Vigdal, E Haande. Ascended from Sweden, N up the long gl., then by the E face. Descended by N ridge. Linked to Swedish top by long ridge.

1b. SE ridge, 900m. Grade IV+. 2 variations of this ridge were climbed by Aberystwyth University Expedition in 1980. The rock was reported as very loose. Ascended via Vestertoppen to camp base in the rocks at foot of ridge proper. Scrambling on loose rock for first 600m. After this one variation followed 200m. buttress direct, pitches up to IV+. The other way took a large cleft 20m. L of main ridge, pitches up to V-. Easier knife-edged ridge followed until awkward, slabby and exposed gap before summit.

SULITELMA 1840m.
2. The northern and highest Swedish top. SE face and the Swedish

Stuorajaekna gl. approach, grade I. 1st ascent 1868, E G Elowson and party.

STORTOPPEN 1822m.

3. The summit dominating the W flank. Normal route by N/NE ridge from approach along N arm of Sallajiekna gl. Mainly walking with some grade I. 1st ascent 1888, E Aanderud and party.

4. Connected to Vardetoppen (1722m.) by one km. very narrow and jagged ridge, probably grade III. 1st ascent 1891, J T Dahl and party.

The most southerly Swedish peak of Sulitelma (1607m.) received a very early ascent by the Swedish botanist G Wahlenberg in 1807.

BLÅMANNEN 1571m.

5. The highest nunatak top, situated on the W edge of the Blåmannsisen ice-cap. The easiest approach is from the S via Kobbertoppen and over the ice-cap. 1st ascent 1891, O Aanderud, W Myhre.

Tysfjord

The Folla coastal sector has been included in the Tysfjord sub-area, as it presents a number of sensational rock walls and towers. The whole sub-area contains many mountains; probably all have been climbed, but details, in particular gradings, are scarce.

Kjerrongøy island, 30 km. N of Bodø, has climbing on several peaks.

VESTRE STRANDÅTIND 712m.

6. 1st ascent 1889, C Hall, M Soggemoen, climbing the NW ridge, about grade III.

STORE STRANDÅTIND 862m.

7a. 1st ascent 1912, H Jentoft, C W Rubenson, F Schjelderup by traverse from Vestre Strandåtind (712m.). Ungraded but climbing up to IV+ with a crux pitch of 20m.

7b. NE ridge, grade IV. 1st ascent 1912, W C Slingsby and party.

The Sørfold mainland district holds another mountain group.

HUSBYVIKTIND 806m.

8. A smooth dome and tower. W ridge ascended 1913 by W Eger, R Løchen, S Saxlund, H Tønsberg. Grade not known but believed hard.

The Nordfold district also has many opportunities with several summits over 1000m. height, some remaining unnamed.

The main part of Tysfjord can be divided into several groups, with a large number of potential routes.

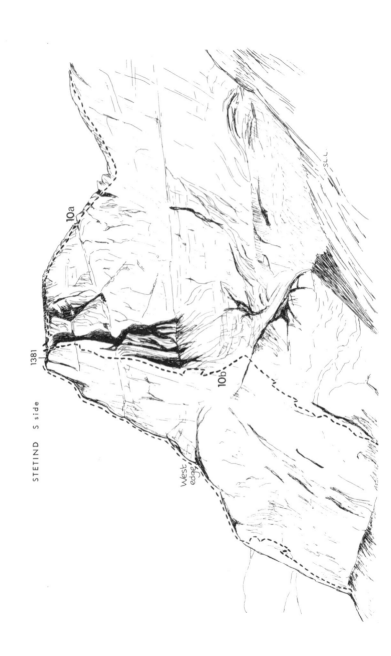

STETIND S side

1381

10a

10b

West edge

SLL

TILTHORN   592m.
   9. An impressive tower with a knife-edge 100m. long summit ridge.

STETIND   1381m.
Superb rock pyramid with several fine climbs. Famous northern land-
mark; has featured on postage stamps; the flanks are smooth rock walls
of 1200m.
   10a. SE ridge (Sydpillaren). Original route, mainly grade II, but
grade IV in one part. 1st ascent 1910, C W Rubenson, A B Bryn and
F Schjelderup. From camp at Storelv go up to shoulder on S arête in
4h. Beyond the long ridge saddle 2 ridge steps of 8-9m. are turned
by ledge system on W side which finishes in a narrow, sloping crack
leading back to main ridge. This necessitates a difficult and exposed
hand traverse (1 h.). Hand traverse was discovered in 1904 by Collie
and the Slingsbys who were turned back by wind and cold.

   10b. S Pillar, 480m., grade V+. Arne Naess and party in 1935.
There are a number of more modern climbs graded up to VI+.

FROSTISEN   1724m.
   11. Peak and gl. are situated S and W of Skjomen fjord. From a
base camp at S end of Storvatnet (S of Mo i Rana on route 50). Go E
up narrow, heavily vegetated valley into corrie. Using a subsidiary
camp below ridge leading E from pt.787m., go over moraine to gl.,
probably small crevasses. Take spur running in direction of pt.1305m,
loose boulders, then snow to final summit rock. 3½h. from subsidiary
camp.

Narvik

It is difficult to determine a boundary between the Tysfjord and Narvik
mountain districts; the mountains merge. Storsteinfjellet (1893m.), the
highest in the area, is shown as 1901m. on older surveys; a large, complex and heavily glaciated mountain with several tops, it lies SE of
Narvik.

STORSTEINFJELLET S top   1872m.
   12. Northern gl. and NW ridge, grade I/II. From a base to the N
go onto the northern part of the gl. (marked as Sealggajiekna) and up
to a col (c.1500m.) on the NW ridge. Follow the ridge, boulders at
first then fine scrambling on good rock, followed by walking with snow
probable. Final short, steep section of scrambling and easy climbing
(II) with slabs and walking to summit (5h.). Descend the same way.
   Continuation NE to main summit involves an initial abseil of 30m.
The remainder of the ridge is believed to have some difficult climbing,
possibly up to IV.

Immediately E of Narvik and easily reached is a small group of peaks.

ROMBAKSTØTTA 1230m.

13. The most northerly peak and perhaps the most popular. The normal route is a fine walk and leads up Tottdalen past lake 819m. and via the E ridge to the summit in 5h. Descent the same way, 4 h.

KONGSBAKKTIND 1575m.

14. Known locally as the Sleeping Queen. It is situated S of Narvik at the head of Skjomdalen, but easily seen from the town. The normal route, believed to be a walk, goes from lake Nervatnet, heading SW past Peppartuva and up the E flank to the ridge. This is followed S to the summit. There are several climbing routes on this mountain, including a complete ridge traverse.

Samer snow scooter and tent

Lofoten & Vesterålen Islands

THIS famous Arctic archipelago curves away from Narvik westwards for 150 km. into the Norwegian Sea in a rugged and mountainous series of islands, progressively diminishing in size. Fittingly, the highest summit, Møysalen (1266m.), rises on the largest island, Hinnøy. There are a great number of smaller but very distinctive mountains on virtually all the islands. Although none are significant in height terms, their sheer granite walls often rising from sea level give an impression of much greater height.

Despite being on or near the Arctic Circle the islands are warmed by an arm of the Gulf Stream, producing a remarkably mild climate. However it is cloudy, wet and windy with the stormiest weather in the western islands, where it can rain over 300 days in a year. It is also possible to have a long dry spell in summer.

The whole group is separated from the mainland, just N of Narvik, by the Tjeldsund. Simplified, the Vesterålen group lies to the N and E in the archipelago, the Lofoten group to the S and W. In detail the border is difficult to define; some islands such as Hinnøy and Austvågøy are partly in each group.

The mountains mainly consist of granite and other volcanic rocks. This does produce some excellent rock in places, but extreme weathering has resulted in large areas of poor or suspect rock. There are a number of small gl., believed to be shrinking in size rapidly. The lower slopes of some islands are covered in dense scrub - mainly birch and large ferns - which can make approaches to climbs very trying. Where the vegetation is rich there can be problems with mosquitoes.

The waters around the islands teem with fish and other marine life; and seals, otters and even occasional whales can be seen. Some of the cliff nesting seabird colonies are colossal; those on Vaerøy once numbered several million birds. Sadly numbers have diminished in recent years due to heavy commercial fishing for sand eels and for other reasons, but they are still a magnificent spectacle.

APPROACHES

The coastal express (Hurtigruten) serves the islands well, arriving daily from Bergen to Stamsund (69 h.); Svolvaer (71 h.); Stokmarknes (75 h.);

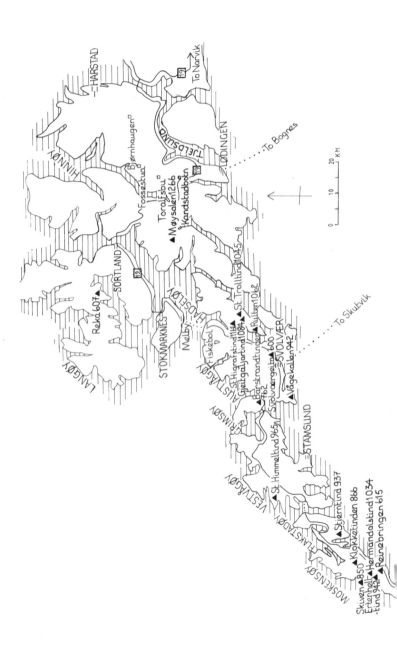

Sortland (77 h.) and Harstad (83 h.). There are onward links by bus and local ferries.

By rail from Oslo to Fauske ($18\frac{1}{2}$ h.). Summer link by Nord-Norge bus to Bognes (3 h.) or Narvik (5 h) where onward links can be made to the islands. By rail from Gothenburg right through Sweden, finally using the historic iron ore line from Luleå to Narvik (26 h.).

With a car, take the E6 all the way to Bognes (1401 km.), car ferry to Lødingen; or Skutvik (1416 km.), car ferry to Svolvaer; or Narvik (1475 km.). In recent years links between the islands have been greatly improved by road extensions and new bridges. From Narvik route 19 continues for another 67 km. to the bridge for Hinnøy island. Then this continues W, linking Langøy and Hadseløy islands by bridges - a further 146 km. Ferry from Melbu to Fiskebol on Austvågøy island (11 km.). Route 19 continues its meandering way, linking Gimsøy and Vestvågøy by bridges - a further 106 km. Short ferry across the Nappstraumen to Flakstadøy, then Moskenesøy; the road finishes at Moskenes in a final 53 km. (1847 km. from Oslo via Narvik).

STARTING POINTS AND BASES

It is difficult to recommend bases and/or starting points for the whole chain. However, there are 7 major islands with important mountain ascent opportunities: Moskenesøy, Flakstadøy, Vestvågøy, Gimsøy, Austvågøy, Hinnøy and Langøy. Major support bases with ferry access from the mainland and all usual facilities are Svolvaer and Lødingen.

MAPS

CAP 400M sh. 4 Central Norway III shows the whole island group and all the final approaches. The 50M survey maps are currently being revised and replaced; all are planned to be fully modernised by 1988.

1031 I	Eggum		1232 I	Kvaefjord
1031 II	Flakstad		1232 II	Gullesfjorden
1031 III	Moskenesøy		1232 III	Sortland
1131 I	Oddvaer		1232 IV	Myre
1131 II	Kabelvåg		1233 I	Andenes
1131 III	Stamsund		1233 II	Overberg
1131 IV	Kvalnes		1233 III	Langenes
1132 I	Nykvag		1332 III	Tjeldsundet
1132 II	Stokmarknes		1332 IV	Harstad
1132 III	Skarvagen		1830 I	Lofotodden
1231 I	Lødingen		1830 III	Vaerøy
1231 IV	Raftsundet			

HUTS and other accommodation

There are few mountain huts of the type found in the mainland system. This is partly because of the lack of continuous upland and partly the short approach distances to the mountains. On Hinnøy there are 3 locked unstaffed huts. Keys and details from the operators: Harstad Turlag, Torvet 7, 9401 Harstad.

Bjørnhaugen	12 beds	map 1332 III	ref. 56-17
Fossestua	8	1232 II	43-14
Toralfsbu	8	1232 II	38-05

Elsewhere there are numerous simple fishermens' huts, known as rorbuer, which can be rented. Also YH at Svolvaer, Andenes, Bo and Melbu. An alternative is to camp and this is often best or even the only means of accommodation within easy access to some of the peaks, particularly on the smaller and more remote islands.

WALKING TOURS

A short tour on Hinnøy using the huts: Harstad to Kanstadbotn in 3 to 5 days (possible ascents en route). Harstad – Bjørnhaugen – Fossestua – Toralfsbu – Kanstadbotn. There is scope for backpacking tours on most islands, using the maps and your own initiative.

ASCENTS

Many routes exist and almost certainly all summits have been ascended. Full details and accurate gradings are often not available. Notes are given island by island, commencing in the W.

Moskenesøy

A remarkably mountainous and heavily indented island with scores of individual summits, some with complex ridges.

HERMANDALSTIND 1034m.

1a. Highest summit. SE ridge, ungraded, believed scrambling. 1st ascent 1900, survey party from Fors fjord. Gain ridge by steep grass slopes to S of pt.539m. Follow ridge with some boulderfields and a 5m. wall to summit, 3h.

1b. N ridge, ungraded, but some climbing. 1st ascent 1903, W C Slingsby, J N Collie and party from Fors fjord via pt.808m. and the spectacular gap in the N ridge, 4h.

1c. Long and difficult connecting ridge to Ertenhelltind (942m.). First traverse not known, but several failed attempts on record.

ERTENHELLTIND 942m.

2. Impressive peak with sharply indented E ridge; by this ridge, ungraded, but probably III. 1st ascent 1903, W C Slingsby, J N Collie and party.

SKIVEN 850m.

3. SW ridge, walking and scrambling. From col at head of Bures fjord, grid ref. 154414. Ascend W flank to obvious bowl. From its centre ascend slabs to a grass terrace, then traverse R past snowfield to SW ridge. Follow ridge direct to summit.

SOLBJØRN 747m.

4. SE ridge, grade I/II. From road at grid ref. 235406 ascend SE ridge with occasional diversions onto E flank. Ascend L branch of a gully and scramble up ridge steeply; easier slabs before summit, 3h.

REINEBRINGEN 615m.

5. Central point of a horseshoe ridge round lake Reine. S ridge, ungraded. 1st ascent 1906, K S Klingenberg and party.

KLOKKETINDEN 866m.

6. A complex of summits and ridges giving a wide variety of climbing. Store Klokketind (866m.), W ridge from nearby Tretinder, via Rubicon Skar, believed grade IV. 1st ascent 1910, A B Bryn, F Schjelderup.

Flakstadøy

One of the smaller main islands but very rocky.

STJERNTIND 937m.

7. Highest summit. N face, short and steep, reputed grade V. 1st ascent 1930, A R Heen and party from Stjernhodet.

Vestvågøy

Rather pastoral compared to other islands, but still with some climbing.

STORE HIMMELTIND 965m.

8. Highest summit. S ridge via Midtre Himmeltind (934m.), ungraded. 1st ascent 1902, H S Mundahl, T G Ouston, coming up from lake Morkedal by col to S of ridge.

Gimsøy

Smallest and least significant island. Interest is centred on a long ridge with numerous summits, called the Barstrandtinder, highest pt.762m.

Austvågøy

Considered by many the best island for climbing. The Trolltinder group lies in the E as a complex of ridges and summits.

STORE TROLLTIND 1045m.

9. E face, ungraded. 1st ascent 1890, M Jeffrey with 2 porters from Trollfjord lake.

STORE HIGRAFSTIND 1161m.

10. SW ridge normal route, ungraded, probably scrambling. 1st ascent 1901, J N Collie, G Hastings and party. From road junction at grid ref. 895825 go up to shoulder through birchwood, take green tongue ascending R and zigzag through small cliffs to boulder slope; finally a gully on L to col. Go up ridge on L directly to first summit. Descend R to large ledge, continue R, round summit block until 2nd chimney on L gives 30m. scrambling to top, 3h. Descend the same way, 1½h.

GJEITGALJARTIND 1084m.

11. NW ridge, walk and scramble. 1st ascent 1910, A B Bryn, C W Rubenson, F Schjelderup. From the end of the Liland road walk along path almost until the head of Østpollen. Ascend through birch forest towards prominent gully lying to L of summit and pinnacles. Go up steep gully, partly snow, to gain corrie gl. above. Cross this and scramble to N ridge which is followed to summit, 3h. Descend same way, 2h.

SVOLVAERGEITA (SVOLVAER GOAT) 600m.
Famous pinnacle overlooking Svolvaer, rising about 330m. above the town. Twin horns (Storhorn, Litlehorn) form the summit. Tradition to jump from high to low, about 5ft. across and 2ft. down.

12. E wall normal route, about 50m. climbing; grade IV at top. 1st ascent 1910, A B Bryn, C W Rubenson, F Schjelderup. Leave road 100m. down from cemetery, path on R of small quarry. Ascend steeply through birchwood, take R fork and go up grass gully to gap. Start climbing from the "neck" between pinnacle and mountain. Begin below the shoulder and climb, first R steeply, then slabs to platform after 13m. Now up steep cracks to shoulder. Traverse onto Svolvaer face and go up steep slab delicately to highest horn. Descend by an abseil to shoulder or further.

VÅGEKALLEN 942m.
Famous complex of ridges and walls in extreme SW of the island.

13a. S face normal route, grade I/II. 1st ascent 1889, M H Ekroll, A Johannessen. Follow valley between Kvanndalstind and Vågekallen. Head for prominent square-cut pinnacle on W ridge. Follow ridge, knife edged in places, till it becomes steep; then take obvious ledge towards broken S face which is followed to top, 3h. Same way down.

13b. E ridge, believed to be grade IV. 1st ascent 1940, A R Heen, L Hansen. An indirect route mostly along the ridge, avoiding difficult bits mainly on the L side. Ascent, 4h.

RULTEN   1062m.
Once described as the finest of Lofoten peaks. It consists of 2 tops, the Austre (1062m.) and Vestre (1035m.), separated by a deep gap.

14. E ridge, reputedly an excellent climb, grade III/IV. 1st ascent 1903, J N Collie, W C Slingsby and party. Best approached from the farm at Reknes. The route consists of slabs, cracks and chimneys in the lower parts, followed by a large tower, then smaller tower. Final traverse on N flank to avoid overhanging section. Descend the same way, several abseils. Round trip, 15h. There are several other routes including a big N face, varying from grade II to V.

Hinnøy

This is the largest island in Norway with an area of 2200 sq. km.

MØYSALEN   1266m.
Double-pointed summit, highest in the islands, situated in the SW.

15. W ridge normal route, probably I/II. 1st ascent not known. From N shore of Lonkan fjord, near Norbotn, go E up the valley, at first along an old miners track, eventually to the col between Lonkan fjord and Indefjorden. Head N, skirting valley flank before aiming for foot of Møysalen gl. The gl. is followed easily to where loose gullies give access to W ridge. Follow up rocky steps with a little climbing, and sometimes a snow ridge, to summit.

Langøy

REKA   607m.
16. A spectacular obelisk. W face, ungraded climbing. 1st ascent 1902, H S Mundahl, T G Ouston. Other routes include NNW face, NW face and SW ridge. Few details but harder than original route.

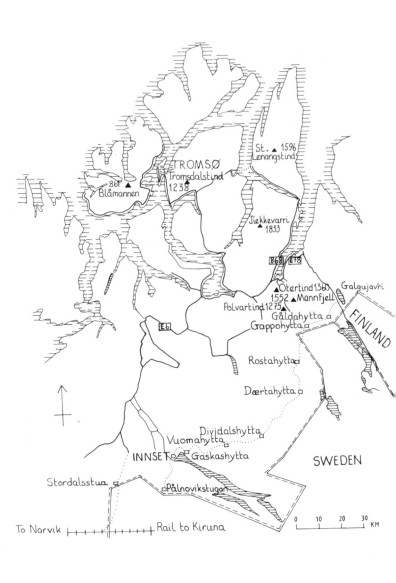

TROMSØ

St. ▲ 1596
Lenangstind

861 ▲
Blåmannen

ᴦ Tromsdalstind
1238

Jiekkevarri
1833 ▲

868/E78

Otertind 1360
1552 ▲ Mannfjell

Galgujavri

FINLAND

Polvartind 1275 ▲
Gåldahytta ᴒ
Gappohytta

E6

Rostahytta ᴒ

Dærtahytta ᴒ

SWEDEN

Dividalshytta ᴒ
Vuomahytta ᴒ
INNSET ᴒ Gaskashytta

Stordalsstua ᴒ

Pålnovikstugan ᴒ

To Narvik ├┼┼┼┼┼┼┼┼┼┼┤ Rail to Kiruna

0   10   20   30
└──┴──┴──┴──┴──┴──┘
                    KM

Troms & Lyngen

ALTHOUGH this is geographically one area, the mountains of the Lyngen peninsula have attracted such interest that they are treated as a separate district. The province of Troms has a tremendous variety of scenery, almost a miniature Norway in itself. Rocky islands, large and small, sea-cliffs and pinnacles, the savagely spectacular gl. and high mountains of Lyngen, whose highest point Jiekkevarri (1833m.) is less than 13km. from the sea. Just inland in the Storfjord district lie lower but hardly less dramatic mountains, including the famous spire of Otertind (1360m.).

Further inland the western sector or Troms border area has a good network of simple huts passing through a district of less rugged but equally wild mountains. The valleys here are deep and heavily forested with large rivers. Individual summits occasionally exceed 1700m. The E sector is similar, but remote and with only scattered huts.

Because of its northern latitude and exposed western location summers are short and subject to very variable weather. Most summer expeditions have experienced violent and prolonged storms at times; northern and western sectors of Lyngen are thus particularly prone. Despite the relatively modest heights, new snow can fall above 1000m. even in July and August. In contrast a few expeditions have enjoyed long periods of settled weather. Such climatic variations are reflected in the gl. and snowfields which vary in size and condition from year to year. Crevasse disposition changes within the season; sérac falls and avalanches are common in most years. The lower rocks are often clean, but extreme weathering has produced rotten and suspect granite at higher altitudes.

Dense birch scrub with masses of rotting vegetation is a feature of many lower valleys. This can cause a lot of problems in places where there are no established paths. Mosquitoes can be troublesome in the inland areas during July and August.

The area is bounded in the N by the sea; in the W partly by the sea and partly by the E6 road; in the S by the Troms provincial border and part of the meandering national border, firstly between Norway and Sweden, then between Norway and Finland; the E boundary is arbitrary, probably the Troms provincial border being the best.

APPROACHES

The coastal express ship can be taken to Tromsø, but this takes 90 h. Regular flights from Oslo are normally expensive but there are special low rates at times.

By rail from Oslo to Fauske takes $18\frac{1}{2}$ h. The Nord-Norge bus runs from Fauske to Narvik (5 h.) twice daily June to August. By rail from Gothenburg to Narvik takes more than 24 h., but the border stops, eg Riksgransen, Bjørnfjell, can be useful jumping off points for touring the Troms border trail.

Using your own transport makes for a long journey; it remains the only satisfactory method for the Lyngen district. Follow the E6 from Oslo to Narvik (1475 km.). Stay on the E6 all the way to Lyngseidet (a further 333 km.) for the Lyngen district. Slightly shorter distance to access roads for other districts.

STARTING POINTS AND BASES

Tromsø is not a forward base to walk or climb from, but it is an excellent and reasonably accessible centre with all facilities. Numerous camping bases have been used by expeditions in their exploration of the Lyngen and Storfjord districts. The border touring district can be approached from several roads leading S, as well as from the Narvik railway.

MAPS

CAP 400M sh.5 Northern Norway gives a useful overview of the area. Otherwise there are modern 50M survey maps.

1432 I	Bardu	1534 II	Ullsfjord
1432 II	Bonnes	1534 III	Tromsø
1434 II	Tussøya	1632 III	Julusvarri
1532 I	Dividalen	1632 IV	Rostadalen
1532 II	Altevatn	1633 II	Helligskogen
1532 III	Salvasskardet	1633 III	Signaldalen
1532 IV	Kirkesdalen	1633 IV	Storfjord
1533 I	Balsfjord	1634 III	Lyngen
1533 II	Tamokdalen	1634 IV	Lyngstuva

HUTS and other accommodation

All huts in the area are run by Troms Turlag (TT), but some are owned by DNT. All are secured with standard DNT locks. Huts have no provisions and would-be users should also take their own butane gas containers (check size with TT).

Unstaffed huts:	beds	Map No.	4-fig. ref.
Daertahytta	18	1632 IV	64-34
Dividalshytta (DNT)	20	1632 III	52-19
Gappohytta (DNT)	20	1633 III	70-60
Gaskashytta (DNT)	10	1532 III	23-17
Gåldahytta	10	1633 II	80-62
Lappjordhytta	14	1532 III	03-02
Nedrefosshytta	16	1733 I	38-90
Nonsbu	12	1534 II	35-34
Ringvassbu	10	1534 IV	28-55
Rostahytta (DNT)	20	1632 IV	61-48
Sappenhytta	11	1734 III	10-17
Skardvassbu	5	1534 III	30-26
Stordalsstua	10	1432 II	85-07
Trollvassbu	16	1534 II	41-37
Vuomahytta (DNT)	10	1532 II	39-18

WALKING TOURS

1. **Troms Border Trail** (about 8 days)
Galgujav'ri - Gåldahytta - Gappohytta - Rostahytta - Daertahytta - Dividalshytta - Vuomahytta - Gaskahytta - Innset. The trail can be extended to the Swedish border via Lappjordhytta and Stordalsstua, or made even longer by linking it with the Swedish hut system.

2. **Short tour E of Tromsø** (3-4 days)
Tromsø/Tromsdalen - Skarvassbu - Nonsbu - Trollvassbu - Oldervikdalen.

ASCENTS

Tromsø District

Tromsø town, situated on an island, is surrounded by mountains of modest height but impressive appearance. A great number of modern rock routes have been undertaken by climbers from Tromsø Climbing Club in recent years.

TROMSDALSTIND 1238m.

1. A very popular mountain less than 6 km. SE of Tromsø. There are 3 ridges (NW/NE/S) which can easily be ascended from Tromsø in about 5h. All are walking. The S ridge can also easily be ascended in winter. 1st winter ascent on skis 1894, P Sverdrup, the Arctic explorer.

BLÅMANNEN 861m.

On the large island of Kvaløya immediately W of Tromsø. Clean granite with several climbing routes. Its N face is considered one of the hardest routes in N Norway.

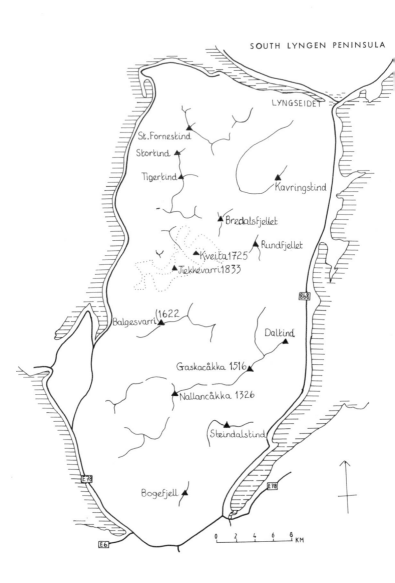

SOUTH LYNGEN PENINSULA

LYNGSEIDET

St. Forneskind
Storkind
Tigerkind

Kavringstind

Bredalsfjellet

Rundfjellet

Kveita 1725

Jiekkevarri 1833

Balgesvarri (1622

Dalkind

Gaskacåkka 1516

Nallancåkka 1326

Steindalstind

868

E78

Bogefjell

E78

E6

0   2   4   6   8 KM

2. E ridge normal route. Easy climbing, grade I/II. From the Kald-fjorden take the path S and follow the ridge to pt.844m., then to the summit, 2-3h.

The island of Kvaløya has many modern technical rock climbs on the extensive granite walls of its numerous small mountains and fjord sides. Detailed information may be obtained from: Tromsø Klatreklubb, PO Box 2777, 9001 Tromsø.

HAMPEROKKEN   1390m.
SE of Tromsø and immediately SE of the broad Breidvikeidet valley.
   3. NW ridge, scrambling. From the road (route 867) take the path along the Tverrelva stream until above the tree-line. Then strike off to the ridge marked as Middags-aksla. This is followed to the summit; very narrow and stony with blocks, about 3h.

   4. Traverse from Hamperokken to Bjørnskardtind (1359m.) and Stortind (1262m.). Fine scrambling and climbing, probably grade I/II. Follow no.3 to summit. Go S and up ridge to Bjørnskardtind without much difficulty. Then go W and descend to col at 1100m. Ascend E ridge of Stortind to summit, total 6-8h.

Lyngen Peninsula

For mountain ascents this is easily the most important and significant district. The peninsula is divided into 2 halves by the Kjosen fjord. The southern sector contains the highest summit, Jiekkevarri (1833m.), and a number of important and difficult peaks. The northern sector culminates in Store Lenangstind (1596m.), and includes many smaller but interesting peaks.

There have been an increasing number of winter ski ascents and winter mountaineering routes in recent years, mainly by local climbers. The weather then is often stable; crevasse and avalanche danger are reduced. The best season is between mid March and mid May.

Southern Sector

JIEKKEVARRI   1833m.

Dominating neighbouring summits by height and bulk; multi-topped, ice-capped, heavily glaciated and with huge rock walls. Complex route finding, and the mountain now has many routes.
   1a. Original route via N ridge of Kveita (1725m.). Scrambling; some snow and ice work. Ungraded. 1st ascent 1897, G Hastings, H Wooley. From Kvalvikdalen ascend to large glacial lake Rypedals-vatn, skirt N shore and ascend scree slopes traversing through a line of crags to get on to the gl, Rypedalsbreen. Ascend steeply W to the col. The N ridge starts here and is followed until about halfway where

it becomes very steep and is turned by crossing from W to E face and up the snow dome, 6h. Descend SW to the col and ascend a broad snow ridge to main summit, 1h.

Descend the same way; or from Austre (E) Jiekkevarri climb down E ridge on excellent rock to where a snow couloir allows an easy descent to the N branch of the Lyngsdal gl. and so into Lyngsdalen.

1b. By Sydbreen gl. and S ridge. Ungraded, mainly scrambling but possibly up to grade III. Axe and crampons. From Lyngsdalen take the track on N bank of Lyngdalselva, walk through forest to Dalbotn, then cross main river (possible campsite), 2h. Ascend to L of wall below Sydbreen, gain lateral moraine and follow to Sydbreen. Go up this gl. easily to upper snow slopes which are ascended directly to rocks of the S ridge. Ascend ridge more or less directly to corniced snow dome; it can be avoided on L. Descend NW slopes of dome to snow basin. Go N to final summit, 7h. Descend same way (7h.) or traverse via Kveita.

1c. W face, ungraded. From Indre Holmbukt follow the Tverrelva stream and go up via the small gl. (grid square 52/08) to the W summit (1668m.). Continue E along the ridge to the main summit. A winter variation of this route exists, ascended mainly on skis, via Blåisen gl. (grid square 53/06).

BALGESVARRI 1622m.

2. A snow and ice dome, rocky to the N. NW face from Lyngsdal Skar, steep scramble. 1st ascent 1899, Mrs E Main and the Imbodens. Approach Lyngsdal Skar from the W via Slokedalen, or longer from the E via Lyngsdalen (involves ascending Sydbreen gl.). From the Skar - col - scramble steeply beside the upper ice of Balgesvarri gl. past pt. 1565m. Continue up ice dome to summit.

NALLANCAKKA 1326m.

3. SW ridge, probably grade II. From a campsite in Steindalen approach the ridge via Steindalsbreen gl., steep in upper section and possibly crevassed. The ridge is believed to be mainly scrambling and some easy climbing up to II.

GASKACAKKA 1516m.

4. W ridge, probably grade III. From a campsite in Steindalen the N flank of the valley is ascended to the col between Gaskacakka and Nallancakka. The W ridge is believed to give 600m. of climbing up to grade III.

Northern Sector

The Jaegervasstind group contains the highest summits of the sector as well as 2 large gl. Store Jaegervasstind (1540m.) used to be considered the highest: 1st ascent 1898, W P Haskett-Smith, Hastings and

Slingsby. They ascended and descended via a gully on the SW face, returning by same route.

STORE JAEGERVASSTIND   1540m.

1. SW ridge, via Lenangsbreen, grade I/II, axe and crampons.
From a campsite at Jaegervatnet village take the track for Kobbenes.
When it ends go E through birch forest to Forholtaksla shoulder. Go up valley between Nordre and Litle Jaegervasstind, then ascend on steep snow, trending R to col. Now descend to upper Lenangsbreen, first traversing E then ascending (avoiding crevasses) to Lenangsskardet col. Descend slightly, traverse W, then ascend upper gl. (crevasses probable) to col between Trolltind and Jaegervasstind. Avoid a 60m. step by traversing R and ascending more easily (I/II). Then follow a broad ridge to final E-W summit ridge. The main summit lies 200m. E, with several easy but exposed rock steps, $8\frac{1}{2}$h. Descent same way in about $5\frac{1}{2}$h.

STORE LENANGSTIND   1596m.

2. Triple summits throwing down jagged ridges. 1st ascent 1898, W P Haskett-Smith, Hastings, Slingsby, Hogrenning by Hasting's Couloir, a wide steep gully on the SW side of the main S ridge. Descended by SE face, contouring round S ridge to Lenangen Skar. NW ridge and Vestre Lenangstind climbed in 1953 by R A Brown, Cook, Faulkner.

TROLLTIND   1425m.

3. S ridge, grade I/II. From Jaegervatnet follow no.1, as far as Lenangsskardet. Now descend slightly and traverse R across gl. and ascend snow to point S of summit. Scramble up intersecting gullies, so gaining summit ridge to R of 1st pinnacle (which forms apex of S and E ridges). Turn 2 gendarmes on R (exposed) and reach 15m. summit block. Traverse L on obvious ledge, then go direct to top (II), 8h. Descend same way, initially by abseil, 6h.

STORE STRUPTIND   1240m.

4. S ridge, grade III. An interesting climb on good rock. From a base in Koppangsdalen get onto Koppangsbreen and traverse across the gl. to adjoining Strupbreen (alternatively, campsite on Strupbreen). The first half of the ridge is easy until a steep step. This is climbed direct up the S edge. The next step is avoided by a traverse R over flakes to a corner. The remainder of the ridge can be taken direct.

PEPPARTIND   1260m.

5. SW ridge. Up to grade IV and gl. crossing. From a base camp at Ytre Gamvik get onto the gl., known as Gamvik-blåisen and traverse SE to a col on the SW ridge of Peppartind. Follow ridge steeply, climbing a series of rock steps (up to IV) to the summit, exposed in places, 9h. Descend the same way.

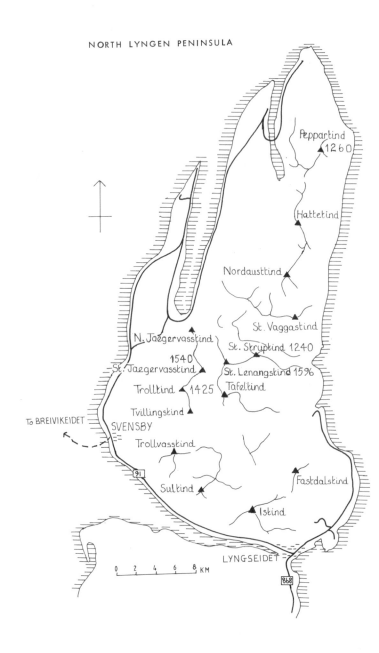

NORTH LYNGEN PENINSULA

Peppartind 1260

Hattetind

Nordausttind

St. Vaggastind

N. Jaegervasstind

1540

St. Struptind 1240

St. Jaegervasstind

St. Lenangstind 1596

Trolltind 1425

Tafeltind

Tvillingstind

To BREIVIKEIDET

SVENSBY

Trollvasstind

Fastdalstind

91

Sultind

Istind

0 2 4 6 8 KM

LYNGSEIDET

868

OTERTIND   1360m.

A sensational pyramid at the head of Signaldalen, with adjacent Litle Otertind (990m.), separated by a narrow cleft known as Hakket. 1st ascent 1911, Endell and Martin from the S.

1. S ridge, probably grade II. From Dalhaug on the E6 follow the path up Mortensdalen; the path then continues up the W flank to the ridge. Climb ridge to summit, 8h.

POLVARTIND   1275m.
2. 1st ascent 1911, K Endell, W Martin, by the N ridge.

MANNFJELL   1552m.
3. 1st ascent 1898, possibly by W ridge, J Caspari.

There is considerable scope for new routes in Signaldalen and in the adjoining valleys, with many impressive corrie walls to explore.

common buzzard

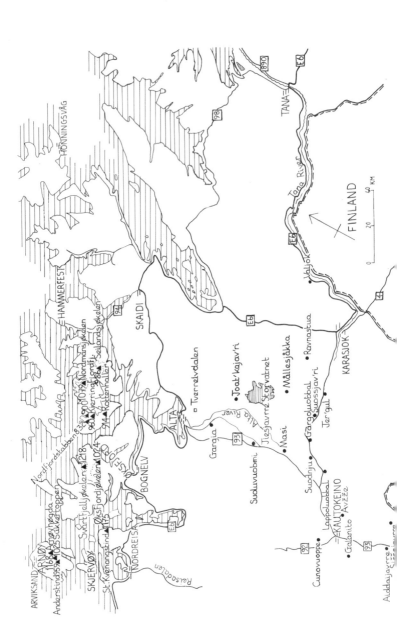

The Far North

THIS is something of an artificial, composite area, constituting the remaining mountain districts of Arctic Norway. The largest part is the vast upland plateau of Finnmark - the most important reindeer supporting and cultural area for the Samer (Lapps), and very much reflected in the remarkable place names. It is an incredible wilderness of more than 22,000 sq. km. There are reputedly more than 42,000 lakes of varying sizes - the largest being Jiesjavrre Storvatnet. In several places the plateau has been deeply dissected by the major rivers of Alta and Tana, along with their important tributaries. Only one road crosses the vidda and summer exploration away from the main tracks has many problems.

There is a well spaced line of state owned small huts, and a marked walking route running Alta - Karasjok - Kautokeino. In winter there are in addition numerous established "snow roads", used by snow scooters and larger snowmobiles, linking the small isolated Samer communities. This means that winter provides the easiest access possibilities and there is excellent ski-touring, particularly during April and early May when days are longer and temperatures less severe. Pure walking tour possibilities are less attractive during the summer months, as walkers can be plagued by mosquitoes. However, late August and September are better in this respect, although winter can return by early October. Combinations of walking with canoe tours and an interest in fishing - especially good - or in wildlife can produce a superb wilderness trip.

In startling contrast to the undulating interior, the rugged islands lying off the NW coast and the Øksfjord peninsula hold small but steep mountains and even 2 significant minor ice-caps. Nordmannsfjord-jøkelen on Seiland island is the most northerly in Scandinavia.

The wildlife of the northern coast, in particular the Varangerfjord district, is very interesting, although fairly thinly spread. High Arctic species such as white-billed diver, king eider and little stint can be found. The vast marshes and multitude of small and large watercourses on Finnmarksvidda hold many interesting wading birds.

Climatically this is approaching true Arctic. The winters are long and hard; even the maritime influence of an arm of the Gulf Stream only affects a few km. inland. Summers are short and cool on the coast, sometimes stormy, although Finnmarksvidda can be very hot at times.

The highest summit is the culminating point of the ice-cap Svartfjell Jøkelen (1218m.) on the Øksfjord peninsula. Finnmarksvidda lies between 700m. and 900m.

The western boundary of the area is in the main the Finnmark/Troms provincial border although the islands and coastal area E of Lyngen fjord will be included; the northern boundary is the Arctic Ocean; the eastern boundary is the featureless wastes leading to the Finnish and Russian borders.

APPROACHES

The coastal express ship can be taken to Hammerfest in $101\frac{1}{2}$h. (more than 4 days). Public transport facilities from here are very limited. There are flights to Hammerfest and Alta, normally expensive, though there are often low summer fares and sometimes special add-on fares from Britain. By rail from Oslo to Fauske takes $18\frac{1}{2}$h. The Nord-Norge bus service runs twice daily June to August and occasionally later. Then from Fauske to Bognelv; to Øksfjord takes 15h. but spread over 3 travelling days.

A more satisfactory method of approach, and for exploration of the area, is to use your own transport. It is a very long and arduous trip through Norway. Follow the E6 from Oslo to Narvik (1475km.). Stay on the E6 to Bognelv (a further 448km.); continue on E6 to Skaidi, then route 94 to Hammerfest (for Seiland island), another 228km.

STARTING POINTS AND BASES

2 have been indicated above; Bognelv for Øksfjord peninsula and Hammerfest for Seiland island. Hammerfest and Alta are useful bases for provisioning and have a range of other services. Alta is particularly important for starting a tour on Finnmarksvidda; other starting points for this plateau involve journeys through Sweden or Finland.

MAPS

CAP 400M sh.5 Northern Norway gives a useful overview of the area. The modern 50M survey maps are:

1634 I	Rotsund	1932 IV	Lavvoai'vi
1634 II	Kåfjord	1933 I	Šuoššjav'ri
1635 II	Arnøy	1933 III	Lappuluobbal
1734 IV	Nordreisa	1933 IV	Masi
1735 I	Silda	1934 II	Iešjavri
1735 II	Oksfjord-jøkelen	1934 III	Suoluvuobmi
1735 III	Olderfjord	1934 IV	Gargia
1832 I	Siebe	1935 IV	Vargsund

1833 II	Kautokeino	2033 IV	Iešjåkka
1835 I	Seiland	2034 III	Stiipanavži
1835 IV	Stjernøya	2134 IV	Rastigai'sa

HUTS and other accommodation

Only Finnmarksvidda has a network of huts. These are all state owned "fjellstuer", normally unlocked and with provisions for sale. They are equipped with cookers and kitchen utensils, but own sleeping bags are required.

	beds	Map No.	4-fig. ref.
Aiddijavrre	8	1832 I	93-28
Avzze	4	1833 II	89-58
Cunovuoppe	4	1833 II	73-63
Galanito	4	1832 I	75-45
Gargia	35	1934 IV	95-46
Gargoluobbal	2	1933 IV	17-95
Jer'gul	8	2033 IV	07-00
Joat'kajav'ri	18	1934 IV	13-41
Kautokeino	38	1833 II	c81-57
Lappoluobbal	14	1933 III	09-80
Masi	5	1933 IV	c04-06
Mållesjåkka	22	1934 II	98-19
Ravnastua	20	2034 III	20-14
Siccajavrre	7	1932 IV	02-29
Suodnju	6	1933 IV	12-10
Suoluvuobmi	32	1934 III	98-22
Šuoššjav'ri	22	1933 I	92-98
Tverrelvdalen	6	1934 IV	94-58
Valljok	8	2134 IV	68-43

WALKING TOURS

1. **Alta to Karasjok** (4-5 days)
Alta - Tverrelvdalen - Joat'kajav'ri - Mållesjåkka - Ravnastua - Karasjok. This tour can be extended to Kautokeino via Jergul and Šuoššajav'ri. Also from Kautokeino it is practical to make your way back to the W coast along a marked trail to Reisadalen and Nordreisa.

Walking away from the hut routes is very much an exploration and complete self-sufficiency is required.

ASCENTS

Arnøy Island

This rugged island lies a little N and E of Lyngen. It can be reached by boat from neighbouring Skjervøy island. Arviksand has shops. The rock is believed to be mainly good granite in the lower parts, but with some loose material higher up.

ARNØYAHØGDA 1168m.
The highest top, situated in the NE and N of Isbakkdalen at the junction of 2 ridges.

1. W face and NW ridge, about 400m., probably mainly grade IV, possibly with a pitch of VI. 1st ascent 1957, E H Hutton, Noble and Thompson. From the W go up Svarttinddalen and into the corrie W of the summit. The W face of the NW ridge is divided by a broad gully with a formidable cliff on R and a ridge on L. A buttress immediately L of the gully forms the route. The crux is about one third way up.

SUKKERTOPPEN 1025m.
2. Lying SW of Isbakkdalen. SE ridge, probably III with a pitch of IV. 1st ascent 1957, E H Hutton, Noble, Treacher. The foot of the ridge is gained from the W via Svarttinddalen and Isbakkdalen. Begins as narrow ridge and merges into face for final 150m. First ascensionists traversed 4 summit peaks and descended via NW ridge.

ANDERSTIND 959m.
3. Unmarked on map but lies between Fosstind (880m.) and Sukkertoppen. Traverse from Sukkertoppen, probably IV, narrow and exposed. 1st ascent 1957, T J C Christie, Gerrard. From Sukkertoppen the main difficulty is a squat overhanging tower, turned on the L by a 2 pitch climb (IV). A rotten pinnacle is avoided on the L, possibly icy. Descent by awkward S ridge to Foss col.

Kvenangen Peninsula

Consists of a main ridge running N–S, with a number of subsidiary ridges mainly W, but also E. Store Kvenangstind (1175m.) is the highest of a group of tops on the main ridge. 1st ascent 1914, C & J Lysholm, by the W face. There are 7 pinnacles on the main ridge. 2 were climbed in 1914 by F & L Schjelderup, the remainder in 1926 by E Fjeld, S Sigvang.

Øksfjord Peninsula

Situated NW of Alta, it holds one medium and 2 small ice-caps with a number of small but impressive mountains. The rock is mainly a good gabbro. On Øksfjord gl. (1204m.) the highest point of the ice is towards the N edge of the ice-cap. 1st ascended 1898, G Hastings and E Høgrenning.

Stjernøy Island

Lies between Øksfjord and Seiland island. Its N coast is deeply indented by fjords. Can be reached by boat from Øksfjord or Hammerfest. Store Kvalfjorddal is a good campsite for S peaks; the head of Smålfjorden for N peaks.

ROTTENHALLER   914m.

1. Easily ascended on S and W sides. NE ridge, ungraded but is climbing. 1st ascent 1956, M J Bayley, D C Ford, B E Swift. From Pollenfjord to top, 3h.

2. E face, N buttress. About 100m., pitches of IV, 3h.

NORDFJORDSTABBEN   832m.

3. E ridge, 200m., pitches of IV. 1st ascent 1956, by the Oxford/Cambridge party.

Further E the parallel ridges of Litle Kjerringfjord fjellet (highest pt. 900m.) and Store Kjerringfjord fjellet (highest pt. 960m.) have both been partly traversed in 1956 by the same party.

Seiland Island

Can be reached by local boat from Øksfjord or Hammerfest. Gyfjorddal is a good campsite for the W; Bekkarfjord for the E.

Seilandstuva (1079m.). This nunatak on Nordmannsjokelen ice-cap is the highest point on the island. It can be ascended easily from the Skreifjord or Bardfjord by its N and W flanks. Its E face is some 3km. in length and between 400 and 550m. high, offering harder climbing possibilities on rock and ice.

The Seiland ice-cap (985m.) is slightly larger and can be ascended easily from any side. 1st ascent 1826, Robert Everest, B M Keilhau.

shore lark

NORTH CAPE, a promontory depicted here in an early 19th century print, and famous as the most northerly projection of Scandinavia and Europe, lies on an island beyond the Far North area coverage in this guide. It presents a 300m. cliff above the sea. Situated about 100km. NE of Hammerfest and 130km. NW of Tana, though much further by road round the fjords, the approach is facilitated by tarmac road and tourist amenities open in summer during the period of the midnight sun. Named from a sighting at sea by Capt. Richard Chancellor in 1553, the cliffs were first climbed in 1899 by K Bing and P Grande – a symbolic gesture – by the N pillar original route, now graded III/IV. Harder routes have been made in recent times.

F. ARCTIC SWEDEN

NARVIK

Tornetrjisk

Abisko

Abiskojaure
Keiron

ToKir

Unna Allakas

Alesjaure

Mårma

NORWAY
SWEDEN

Tjäktja

Vistas

Nallo

Vaktposten 1852 ▲ Unna Räita
Knivkammen 1878 ▲ 1900 ▲ Pyramiden

Sälka

Drakryggen 1831 ▲ ▲ 1990 Kebnepakte
2117 ▲ Kebnekaise

Tolpagornil 662 ▲ Kebnekaise

Singi

Nikkaluokta

0   5   10   15   KM

Kaitumjaure

Kungsleden

Vakkotavare

Kebnekaise

AS the most northerly of the Swedish ranges this area includes the twin summits of Kebnekaise (2117, 2097m.), the highest mountain in Sweden and in Arctic Scandinavia. It is a relatively modest sized, compact group of some 500 sq. km., but includes 200 distinct tops and about 50 small and receding gl. Nevertheless, some parts are fairly remote, and as much as 3–4 days march from the nearest road. The place names and main geographical features are Lappish and remarkably colourful and descriptive. The mountain of Kaskasanjunjetjåkkå (1780m.) probably has the longest name.

Lying about 68 N the climate is virtually high Arctic; summers are short and cool, winters can produce valley snow cover for up to 8 months. Between April and September there are long hours of daylight, with no darkness at all for about 8 weeks. The harsh climate has affected the quality of the rock in some parts. The terrain is characterised by extensive boulder fields, particularly in the upper valleys where camping can be problematical. However, the area has received quite a lot of attention, mainly from Swedish climbers who have produced more than 100 routes of all grades.

The area is bordered in the N by the railway from Luleå to Narvik; in the W by the Norwegian border; in the E by lower ground in the northern sector and the Vistasvagge valley in the southern sector; in the S roughly by the broad Ladtjovagge valley running westwards from Nikkaluokta.

APPROACHES

From Gothenburg by train either to Kiruna (23h.) or Abisko (25h.). By train from Stockholm either to Kiruna (20h.) or Abisko (22h.). With a car from Gothenburg, take the E3 towards Stockholm until Arboga; then the E18, finally route 55 to Uppsala. The excellent E4 Baltic coastal road is now followed past Luleå towards the Finnish border, to take route 98 inland (NW) to Kiruna, and finally W along the surprisingly good road to Nikkaluokta (total about 1900 km.). Or continue from Kiruna along the newly built road to Abisko (about 2000 km.).

BASES

Kebnekaise fjällstation offers accommodation and meals service, with alternative self-service or camping; limited provisions for sale. There are many possible camping bases elsewhere in the range.

MAPS

For the approaches, regional map LB 400M sh.8 Norra Norrland. For detailed navigation LB 100M Nys Fjällkartan series map BD6 Abisko - Kebnekaise gives excellent coverage of the whole area.

HUTS and other accommodation

All huts are run by the Swedish Touring Club (STF). Additional privately owned chalet accommodation at Nikkaluokta.

Staffed huts:	beds	Map No.	Lat./Long.
Abisko	243	BD 6	18.47E/68.22N
Kebnekaise	150	BD 6	18.37E/67.52N
Self-service huts:			
Abiskojaure	43	BD 6	18.35E/68.18N
Alesjaure	78	BD 6	18.25E/68.08N
Kebnekaise Toppstuga	8	BD 6	18.31E/67.53N
Kieron	4	BD 6	18.36E/68.15N
Mårma	4	BD 6	18.46E/68.06N
Nallo	20	BD 6	18.24E/68.02N
Sälka	54	BD 6	18.17E/67.57N
Singi	49	BD 6	18.19E/67.52N
Tarfala	14	BD 6	18.36E/67.54N
Tjäkta	20	BD 6	18.15E/68.03N
Unna Allakas	22	BD 6	18.11E/68.12N
Unna Räita	4	BD 6	18.28E/67.58N
Vistas	20	BD 6	18.36E/68.02N

There are also a number of windshelters providing emergency overnight shelter.

WALKING TOURS

The excellent hut system in the area gives good opportunities for hut to hut walking and ski tours.

1. Kungsleden (Abisko - Singi section)   4-5 days
This famous long distance route begins at Abisko. Abisko - Abiskojaure - Alesjaure - Sälka - Singi - Kebnekaise. It continues S from Singi for a further 350 km. to Ammarnäs, with proposed extensions further S.

2. Abisko - Kebnekaise (mountain route)   6 days
Abisko - Abiskojaure - Alesjaure - Nallo (via the W Passusjietna gl.) -

Unna Räita - Tarfala - Kebnekaise.

3. Kebnekaise circuit   6-7 days
Nikkaluokta (part way by boat) - Vistas - Nallo (2 nights with time to
visit Unna Räitavagge) - Sälka - Singi - Kebnekaise.

Other tours continue N of Abisko into the Troms border area of Norway;
also W into the Narvik area and S into Sarek National Park.

ASCENTS

KEBNEKAISE S top   2117m.
    1a. E face ordinary route. Walk and scramble, grade 1, 4-5h. A
signposted path W from Kebnekaise fjällstation (680m.) rises gradually
to a steep gully with torrent after one km. Ascend this firstly on true L
bank, then R until moraine. Now less steeply to the easy Björlings gl.
Cross gl. W and go up snow ridge abutting on 150m. rock step. Zigzag
up this, loose in places, some fixed ropes, until broad summit ridge.
Turn N and ascend for one km. until final snow dome which can be icy
and narrow. Superb exposed summit with outstanding views. Descend
the same way or via S face route - a steep, stony and rather boring
walk - although interesting on skis.

    1b. N ridge traverse from Kebnepakte (1990m.) via Kebnekaise N
top (2097m.). Classic traverse, grade 2-3 rock, plus ice ridge; 5-6h.
From Tarfala huts (1170m.) ascend steep moraine W to Kebnepasset.
Climb N ridge of Kebnepakte on mainly good rock, several variations
possible. Descend S ridge to interesting rock step (Halspasset). Now
ascend to Kebnekaise N top then follow narrow exposed ridge to S top,
sometimes corniced.

There are more than 20 other routes on the mountain of varying lengths
up to 400m. and graded from 1 to 4. Kebnetjåkkå, a stony plateau N
of the tourist station, is an excellent viewpoint for the main Kebnekaise
massif and its routes. Steep path up from the huts.

DRAKRYGGEN   1831m.
    2. E ridge. Fine scramble, grade 1, 2h. From Tarfala to Kebne-
passet (1480m.) as no.1b above. Go W, descending slightly, take an
ascending traverse line W up the small Pass gl. and finish in a pleasant
snow arête abutting against the rock of the E ridge. This is followed
pleasantly to the summit on mainly good rock.

KASKASAPAKTE   2040m.
A superb peak situated on the N side and dominating the narrow Kebnepasset. Its long classic SW ridge (grade 3) takes a natural and direct
line from the pass. There are other routes of varying difficulty; the N
Pillar is grade 5.

KASKASAPAKTE from SW

2043/2040

SW ridge

S.L.L.

TUOLPAGORNI 1662m.

This impressive, sharp conical rock peak lies only 3km. from Kebnekaise fjällstation and offers virtual crag climbing, with routes of up to
600m. It now has a network of about 10 climbs on mainly excellent
rock, from grade 1 to 6. The most famous is Silhuettleden (4-5), 1st
ascent 1938, E Rossipal, G Santesson. This was the first climb on the
imposing main wall and the chief difficulties are in the first 250m.
Several harder modern routes now use this wall.

A little further N the interesting S wall of the valley of Unna Räitavagge holds several distinctive peaks.

KNIVKAMMEN 1878m.

3. Literally "knife-edge". Ridge traverse SE to W, grade 2-3, 10-
12h. round trip. From Unna Räita hut (1300m.), or camping in upper
Kaskasavagge, go to the Pyramiden-passet; traverse NW onto the ridge
and follow directly to summit (4h.). Traverse W along ridge for $1\frac{1}{2}$km.,
narrow and exposed in places (1-2h.), finally descending S on to the
Kaskasavagge gl. Some loose rock and heavily covered in lichen, can
become very difficult in wet conditions.

VAKTPOSTEN 1852m.

4. NE ridge, grade 2, 3-4h. for ascent. From Unna Räita hut traverse E side of gl. lake to foot of easy Tjäktjahjälmen gl. Ascend this
diagonally to foot of NE ridge. Go up to 1st summit on mixed quality
rock, traversing 3 pinnacles on the narrowing ridge. Traverse S then
W to main summit along a one km. ridge (walking). Descend easily to
S, first on to snowfield, then stony slopes to the gl.

PYRAMIDEN 1900m.

5. W ridge, scramble and walk, 3h. From Unna Räita hut head S,
slightly losing height to start of Pyramiden gl. Follow E flank mainly
to Pyramiden-passet. Follow W ridge easily, mostly broad but with
some steps and narrower sections. Descend the same way.

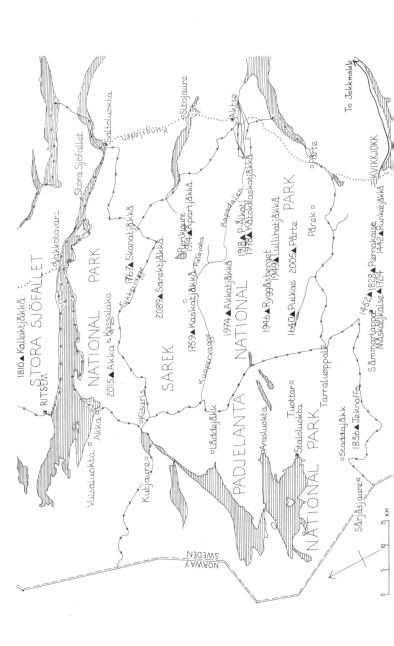

Sarek National Park

ARGUABLY the finest mountain area in Scandinavia, certainly the wildest and least accessible. Promoted as the "last great wilderness" in Europe it has received an increasing number of walkers in recent years, mainly confined to the valleys and easy passes. The total area is almost 2000 sq. km.

There is no hut system and only a few bridges in key locations to reduce river crossing casualties. While regulations keep out cross-country vehicles and prevent commercial exploitation, the walker and climber have unrestricted access and camping. The emphasis is on independent sufficiency and groups must be self supporting in food and equipment - quite a problem for a stay exceeding 2 weeks.

Much has been written about the wildlife of Sarek and the list of bird and mammal species known is impressive. White-tailed sea eagle, golden eagle, gyr falcon, wolverine and brown bear particularly fire the imagination. However the list should be treated with caution as the actual numbers of each species are small; the animals are shy and not easily found.

Above all Sarek is an area of mountains and gl. in a unique (in Europe) wilderness setting. There are more than 250 distinct tops of which 87 are over 1800m. and 8 are over 2000m. Although all summits have now been reached there is considerable scope for new climbing routes of all grades. A visit to Sarek is an expedition. Touring across the park on foot or ski can take a week using the shortest line. River crossings (in summer) are numerous and can be a serious hazard, especially in very wet or very warm weather. Carrying in sufficient equipment for a mountaineering expedition is a major problem. Walking or ski-touring can involve 25kg. rucsac loads; 30kg. or more must be expected by climbers. Mountain rescue can take a long time.

The area is bounded in the N by lake Akkajaure and Stora Sjöfallet National Park; in the E by lower ground and the Kungsleden trail; in the S by a rather arbitrary line linking Tjaktjajaure lake through the Änok delta to the upper Tarraätno valley; in the W the Tarraätno valley and Padjelanta National Park.

RAPADALEN and SKÅRKI GROUP from S

LUOTTO-TJÅKKOK GROUP from SE

APPROACHES

From Gothenburg by train to Gällivare (21 h.), or from Stockholm in
18 h. Then by daily postbus to northern starting points (3–5 h.). From
Gothenburg or Stockholm to Murjek (20 h. or 17 h.), then bus to Kvikkjokk (3½ h.) for southern starting points. Using your own transport,
from Gothenburg take the E3 towards Stockholm until Arboga, then
the E18, finally route 55 to Uppsala. The excellent E4 Baltic coastal
road is then followed virtually to Luleå. Now by route 97 to Jokkmokk
(about 1700 km.). Or, continue from Jokkmokk on route 97 until the
long access road turns off NW along Stora Lulevatten and Akkajaure –
about 1800 km.

BASES

There are no bases with any facilities in Sarek itself, but some food
re-supply is available from the STF Aktse hut at the SE end of Rapadalen.
Provisions are also available at Kvikkjokk.

Within the park there are many possible camp bases for walking and
climbing exploration. Extensive boulder fields produce problems in most
upper valleys. Some recommended climbing bases are:

1. By Pierikjaure lake
2. By Sarekjaurati tarn
3. On Luottolako
4. Upper Sarvesvagge
5. Upper Njåtjosvagge
6. Below Kuoperskaite (in Kuopervagge)
7. Near to the Pårtejekna gl.

MAPS

For the approaches, regional maps LB 400M sh.8 Norra Norrland, and
sh.7 Mellersta Norrland. For detailed navigation, LB 100M in the Nya
Fjallkartan series sh.BD 10 Sareks Nationalpark.

HUTS and other accommodation

Although there are no huts actually in the National Park, the perimeter
contains about 20 huts within the STF system. Several of these are useful
in approaching or leaving Sarek. In addition there are a few small private shelters which are mostly locked. Do not plan to use any of these
while touring.

WALKING AND SKI TOURS

Deep valleys and usable passes abound. With a map it is possible to
plan any number of foot or ski tours. A few suggested routes are:

1. Kvikkjokk – Stuor-tata – Pårek – Säkok – Njåtjosvagge – Staloluokta (Padjelanta)   6–7 days.

KÅTOKTJÅKKÅ from W

UNNA STUOLLO (centre L), PIELLORIEPPE GROUP

2.   Aktse – Rapadalen – Snavvavagge – Pielavalta – Pierikjaure –
Kukkesvagge – Kassalako – Akka (Stora Sjöfallet)   8–9 days.

3.   Sitojaure – Pastavagge – Pielavalta – Skarja – Kuopervagge –
Kisuris – Akka   8–9 days.

ASCENTS

The mountains can be subdivided into 14 small but distinct massifs:
A. Akka-Rita / B.   Kisuris / C.   Lanjek / D.   Luotto-Tjäkkok /
E. Piellorieppe / F.   Pårte / G.   Ruotes / H.   Sarektjåkkå /
I. Sarves / J.   Skierfe-Tjakkeli / K.   Skårki / L.   Tsatsa-Tjuolta /
M. Ålkatj-Tielma / N.   Äpar.   Notable extracts from these are:

A. Akkatjåkkå   1974m.
1. NE ridge, walk. 1st ascent 1896, A Hamberg. From a base in
Alkavagge (c.800m.) cross the valley and river to foot of broad ridge
which is ascended to summit. Descend the same way or S to Sadel-
berget pass and gl.

D. Ryggåsberget   1946m.
2. The highest peak of the massif, easy and with excellent views. SE
flank. 1st ascent March 1926 on ski, H N Pallin. Ascended from a
camp on the large upland plain of Luottolako, firstly over the easterly
top at 1910m.

D. Pulkas   1640m.
Not significant in height but with a dramatic and still unclimbed SW
wall of over 400m.

E. Kåtokkaskatjåkkå   1978m.
3. S ridge (grade 1) and traverse to Kåtoktjåkkå nordtoppen (1928m.),
grade 1–2. From a site below Pårtejekna gl., either follow Kåtokjåkkå
river to gl. and cross snout to N bank, or cross the river (dangerous).
Traverse some 5km. into Jeknavagge and ascend boulders to foot of S
ridge. This is taken directly to summit on mostly excellent rock; ridge
pleasantly narrow towards top. Descend NE, then E, some poor rock.
Traverse along narrow exposed ridge until final 100m. tower. Avoid
first part on R then go direct to summit of nordtoppen. 7–8 h. Descend
SW face, boulders then snow.

E. Piellorieppe   1918m.
Highest point, Ålkatj. An impressive multi-topped mountain towering
over the Rapaselet sector of the Rapadalen valley. Its NE face provides routes of over 1000m.
4a. SW ridge, grade not known, believed scrambling. 1st ascent 1933
C V Andersson, S Astrom. 1st winter ascent in 1942. Can be climbed

MAIN PÁRTE GROUP from SE

LULLIHATJÅKKÅ from E

from a site close to the Rapadalen/Sarvesvagge valley confluence. The route is believed to use the narrow Stuolovagge onto the Stuolojekna gl. and the col at 1547m.

4b. A superb ridge connects all the Piellorieppe tops. This was traversed N-S in 1969 by M & O Ljunggren, grade not known. The tops are: Piellorieppe-Stuollo (1608m.) - Glaciärtoppen (1678m.) - Lilltoppen (1613m.) - Östkam (1828m., 1830m.) - Ålkatj (1918m.).

F. Pårtetjåkkå 2005m.
5. E ridge normal route, a long walk, 5h. 1st ascent 1896, A Hamberg. From a site below Pårtejekna gl. (c.1200m.) traverse tedious boulder field to ridge beyond tiny Pårektjekna gl. Ascend the broad ridge mainly on boulders. Traverse NW, first to the observatory buildings then the summit; excellent views. A more interesting way down traverses further E over Pårektjåkkå (1805m).

F. Lullihatjåkkå 1949m.
6a. SW ridge, original route, walking and scrambling, grade 1-2. 2h. from pass. 1st ascent 1927, O Kjellberg, C A Ullén, S Åström. From foot of Pårtejekna gl. ascend in NW direction for nearly 5km. to pass, mainly bare ice in summer with awkward melt runnels and some dangerous deep holes. The ridge can be taken virtually direct, with some suspect rock and exposed places ; superb summit. Descend the same way.
6b. E ridge, grade 2-3. Believed fine climb. 1st ascent 1980, by B Rodin, B Tengrud. Can be approached from the Pårtejekna gl. to pass at foot of the ridge; or by ascending Lullihatjårro (1586m.) and traversing the easy ridge to same pass. The route is believed to follow the ridge directly, including pinnacles.

G. Kaskatjåkkå 1759m.
7. A rarely visited mountain. N ridge, a walk. 1st ascent 1957, G Borenius, D Nygren, T Persson, S Sundius. From a base in upper Ruotesvagge (c.900m.) get onto the true R bank of the Årjep Ruotesjekna gl., then traverse up to the pass leading to the small lake called Paisajaurati. Take the N ridge direct to the top. Descend same way.

H. Sarektjåkkå 2089m.
The highest summit in Sarek. 1st ascent 1879, cartographer G W Bucht and party, using a variation of the W flank normal route.
8a. W flank normal route. 1st ascent 1895, A Hamberg. From Mikkastugan (840m.) in Ruotesvagge go easily up the E side of Mikkajekna gl. (some crevasses and deep holes). Take upper snowfield and rocks up S flank of W ridge of Stortoppen to summit.
8b. Stortoppen from Sarekpakte (1800m.). Ridge traverse, grade 2-4. From Sarekjaurati lake (989m.), lying NE of the group, head W until the tiny Sarekpakte gl. Follow broad ridge SW to Sarekpakte. Now

a narrow ridge S to Nordtoppen, then SW to Stortoppen.

N. Äpartjåkkå 1914m.
9. S face and ridge, a walk. 1st ascent 1896, A Hamberg. From the Pierikjaure lake (801m.) head SE into Pastavagge which is followed to beneath the S face. Ascend NE to ridge, broad at first; follow to the summit.

short-tailed vole

Padjelanta & Stora Sjöfallet National Parks

THERE are many thousands of sq. km. of upland in Sweden N of the Arctic Circle. Much of it is in the nature of rolling fells, liberally interspaced with large and smaller lakes. The tree line reaches over 700m. in places and there are great expanses of upland bogs and mires. Much of this vast region is little known or used, except by the native Samer (Lapp) people. Two districts, Padjelanta and Stora Sjöfallet, are sufficiently distinctive and interesting to have achieved a definite identity as National Parks, fascinating for their mountain beauty and wildlife, and equipped with huts for walking and ski tours. Together with the adjoining Sarek and Muddus National Parks, the Sjaunja Bird Sanctuary and the Tjuoltavuobme Forest Reserve they form the largest preserved wilderness area of Europe (8405 sq. km.).

Padjelanta, stretching to the Norwegian border, takes the form of an upland plateau containing several very large and outstandingly beautiful lakes, with mainly isolated mountains; Jeknaffo (1836m.) is the highest. Stora Sjöfallet is more mountainous, to a great extent providing the catchment area for Stora Sjöfallet (The Great Waterfall) itself. Ironically this incomparable waterfall has now been effectively destroyed by hydro-electric developments. The impressive, multiple topped Akka (2015m.) is the highest mountain. Other mountains lie just outside the National Parks but form an integral part of the area. The Tarrekaise massif is the most significant, effectively forming a 15 km. wall on the E side of Tarradalen, N of Kvikkjokk. The higheast top is Piernakaise (1828m.).

Forming part of the mountain boundary between maritime and continental climates the weather can be very variable. Nevertheless the winters are long and cold; January mean temperatures are between -20C and -24C, but with milder spells. Summers are generally cool; the July mean is between 10C and 12C with a considerable amount of rain in July and August.

The western boundary of Padjelanta is the Norwegian border; its eastern boundary is the Sarek National Park; northern and southern limits are not easy to define, but are clearly shown on maps. Stora Sjöfallet western boundary is mainly Sarek National Park; the other boundaries are difficult to define, but are also shown on maps.

APPROACHES

From Gothenburg by train to Gällivare (21 h.), or from Stockholm (18h.). Then by postbus to starting points in Stora Sjöfallet and finally for Padjelanta (3-5 h.). Or, from Gothenburg or Stockholm to Murjek (20 h. or 17 h.), then bus to Kvikkjokk (3½ h.) for southern starting points in the Padjelanta.

With a car from Gothenburg, take the E3 towards Stockholm as far as Arboga, then the E18 and finally route 55 to Uppsala. The excellent E4 Baltic coastal road is then followed virtually to Luleå. Then take route 97 to Jokkmokk, finally the high quality minor road to Kvikkjokk (about 1700 km.). Alternatively, continue from Jokkmokk on route 97 until the long access road turns off NW along Stora Lulevatten and the Akkajaure (about 1800 m.).

STARTING POINTS AND BASES

The area is best suited to backpacking or ski-touring and there are no appropriate bases for overall exploration. Starting points are numerous for Stora Sjöfallet all along the road from Gällivare to Ritsem. Kvikkjokk in the S and Ritsem in the N are the best.

MAPS

For the approaches, LB 400M regional map sh.8 Norra Norrland and sh.7 Mellersta Norrland. For detailed navigation, LB 100M in the Nya Fjällkartan series are excellent:

BD 7 Akkajaure-Sitasjaure   BD 10 Sareks nationalpark
BD 8 Kebnekaise-Saltoluokta BD 12 Staloluokta-Sulitelma-Kvikkjokk
BD 9 Vaisaluokta-Saltoluokta

HUTS and other accommodation

Huts in Stora Sjöfallet are run by the Swedish Touring Club (STF). Huts in Padjelanta are run by STF and Naturvårdsverket (SNV) and are all self-service.

Padjelanta	beds	Map No.	Lat./Long.
Arasluokta	32	BD 9	16.48E/67.23N
Kisuris	34	BD 9	17.12E/67.34N
Kutjaure (STF)	20	BD 9	17.02E/67.36N
Låddejåkk	28	BD 9	16.54E/67.28N
Staddajåkk	12	BD 12	16.36E/67.15N
Staloluokta	36	BD 12	16.42E/67.19N

Såmmarlappa (STF)	18	BD 12	17.09E/67.04N
Sårjåsjaure (STF)	14	BD 12	16.29E/67.14N
Tarraluoppal	36	BD 12	17.07E/67.12N
Tuottar	38	BD 12	17.02E/67.16N

Stora Sjöfallet
Staffed hut: Saltoluokta	74	BD 10	18.31E/67.24N
Self-service huts: Akka	40	BD 9	17.22E/67.38N
Vaisaluokta	20	BD 9	17.16E/67.41N
Vakkotavare	20	BD 10	18.06E/67.36N

Lying just outside the National Parks but forming an integral part of the network are several other huts.

Self-service huts:
Aktse	34	BD 10	18.18E/67.09N
Njunjes	20	BD 10	17.25E/66.57N
Tarrekaise	30	BD 10	17.18E/66.59N

WALKING ROUTES AND ASCENTS

Padjelanta has a particularly fine through route N-S, which is equally good in either direction; easy walking or, in winter, ski-touring in a true wilderness setting.

Kvikkjokk to Ritsem   (about 12 days)
Kvikkjokk - Njunjes - Tarrekaise - Såmmarlappa - Tarreluoppal - Tuottar - Staloluokta - Arasluokta - Låddejåkk - Kutjaure or Kisuris - Vaisaluokta or Akka - Ritsem. Several variations can be taken away from the N-S axis; further W into Norway or E into Sarek Nat. Park.

Stora Sjöfallet is something of an intermediate touring area. The huts are located as continuations of longer through routes such as Padjelan-taleden and Kungsleden. Stora Sjöfallet is also often used as the start of walking or ski tours into Sarek and canoe tours into Sjaunja nature reserve.

There are a number of interesting individual mountains most of which attract few ascents. However the northern part of the park is domina-ted by the huge multi-topped mountain of Akka (2015m.), almost a massif in itself.

AKKA Stortop 2015m.
  1. Hyllglacier and N face. Walking and gl. crossing with some crevasse risk, and snow slopes. 1st ascent 1900, S Ekman, N Flygare,

B Söderborg. From the Akka huts, or much more easily from a campsite on the southern shore of Akkajaure, get to the true R bank of the Njir-amjåkkå and ascend steeply, following the L fork to the Hyllglacier, not direct to the Hambergs gl. Ascend the gl. then take a line up the snowfield and stony slopes to the summit, 5-6h. from Akkajaure, and at least 2h. more from the Akka huts.

There are walking and scrambling routes on all the Akka tops - in order of height: Borgtoppen (1963m.), Dubbeltoppen (1830m., 1820m.), Manstoppen (1780m.), Västtopparna (1780m., 1734m.), Sunnatjåkkå (1765m.), Nummertoppen (1760m.), Maudtoppen (1680m.), Mattotjåkkå (1676m.), Majtoppen (1628m.), Apriltoppen (1604m.).

SKANATJÅKKÅ 1767m.

2. N flank, an easy walk. Lying some 20km. SE of Akka, it is best ascended in 3-4h. from a campsite in upper Kukkesvagge. Excellent views of the Sarekjåkkå and Äpar groups.

KALLAKTJÅKKÅ 1810m.

3. This multi-topped peak is the highest of the little visited mountains lying NE of Akkajaure lakes. S flank and ridge, a walk. Start from the road to Ritsem either before or after the Raivotjåkkå hill (1405m.). Ascend flank to foot of S ridge which is followed to summit without problems. Outstanding views.

Immediately SE of Padjelanta the Tarrekaise massif has some obvious possibilities but few recorded ascents. From the map a grand traverse N-S of some 12km. looks feasible, to include most peaks from Såmm-artjåkkå (1452m.) to Runkatjåkkå (1442m.).

Set slightly apart from the others, Måskatjkaise (1742m.) projects an impressively steep 1100m. S ridge rising from Tarradalen. The whole E wall of Tarradalen offers some climbing possibilities.

wolverine

APPENDIX 1

ENGLISH BIBLIOGRAPHY

A number of books and booklets in English have been issued in Norway by various bodies; all except one are long out of print. Hundreds of articles on Norway and Sweden have been published in British journals and magazines over a period of nearly 150 years – they are too numerous to list here. Apart from publications in the Scandinavian tongues few works have been issued in other languages. In Western Europe an attitude prevails that the traveller expects to find specialist works about the Scandinavian mountains in English only.

J.D. Forbes. Norway and its Glaciers visited in 1851. A & C Black, Edinburgh. 1853.

W.C. Slingsby. Norway – The Northern Playground. David Douglas, Edinburgh. 1904. Notably re-issued by Basil Blackwell, Oxford, in 1941.

Le Blond, Mrs Aubrey. Mountaineering in the Land of the Midnight Sun. T. Fisher Unwin, London. 1908.

T. Weir. Camps and Climbs in Arctic Norway. Cassell, London 1953.

P. Prag. Mountain Holidays in Norway. Norway Travel Association, Oslo. 1970.

A. Howard. Walks and Climbs in Romsdal. Cicerone Press, Milnthorpe. 1970.

E. Nilsson. Sarek (Laplands wild-life sanctuary). Interbook, Stockholm. 1971.

E. Welle-Strand. Mountain Touring Holidays in Norway. Norway Travel Association, Oslo. 1974. Partly updated 1981.

APPENDIX 2

MAPS

Cappelen maps (CAP) referred to throughout the guide are issued under various covers which gives the impression that different versions may be available. This is not the case; irrespective of covers, their titles, sub-titles etc. the maps are identical in the overlapping grid of five sheets and the content of each is the same. The three commonest cover versions correspond with each other as follows:

1-2	Sør Norge – sor	1.	Southern Norway – South
3-4	Sør Norge – nord	2.	Southern Norway – North
5-6	Møre og Trøndelag	3.	Møre and Trøndelag
7-8	Norland	4.	Nordland
9-10	Troms og Finnmark	5.	Troms and Finnmark

1 Southern Norway (Oslo – Stavanger – Bergen)
2 Central Norway I (Oslo – Bergen – Ålesund)
3 Central Norway II (Ålesund – Trondheim – Namsos)
4 Central Norway III (Brønnøysund – Bodø – Narvik)
5 Northern Norway (Tromsø – Hammerfest – Kirkenes)

Other language versions (eg German) of the latter set of 5 exist. The first 3 sheets are 325M scale, the last 2 are 400M.

A recent commercial competitor to CAP is mapping published in West Germany under the marketing name of Terrac. This comes in 7 sheets over virtually the same ground as CAP. We refrain from commenting about the comparative merits of the two, as further changes are likely.

1 300M Southeastern Norway (Oslo and surrounding region)
2 300M Southwestern Norway (Stavanger, Bergen and region)
3 300M Eastern Norway and Southern Trøndelag
4 300M Western Norway
5 300M Trondheim and surrounding region
6 400M Northern Norway
7 400M Finnmark and Tromsø

The Swedish National Survey (SL) have now (March 1987) integrated the Liber (LB) New Mountain Series maps into their own (new) series of Mountain Maps. All new maps are now published by SL, although the former LB ones are likely to remain in use for a long time.

This has resulted in some numerical and name changes, but 11 of the 31 original LB index retain the same numbers and names.

For this guide, note the following changes:

Area 12	BD 15 becomes	26FG	Vuoggatjålme
	BD 16	25G	Ammarnäs
	AC 1	25EF	Umfors
	AC 3	24EF	Tärnaby
	AC 4/5	23EF	Fatmomakke
	Z 1	22E	Frostviken
	Z 2	22F	Risbäck
	Z 3	21E	Håkafot
Area 14	BD 12	27G	Sulitelma
Area 20	BD 7	29GH	Sitasjaure
	BD 9	28G	Virihaure
	BD 12 becomes	27G	Sulitelma

The new SL mountain maps have been revised as regards marked paths, shelters, huts etc. All other Swedish map numbers/names remain unchanged.

Index